CAN I TRUST THE BIBLE as GOD'S WORD?

HOW DO I KNOW?
WHAT IS THE EVIDENCE?

BY DR. RUTH TANYI

Can I Trust The Bible As God's Word? How Do I Know? What Is The Evidence?
Copyright © 2017 by Dr Ruth Tanyi.
Published by   Dr Ruth Tanyi Ministries, Inc
                  P O BOX 1806
                  Loma Linda, CA, 92354, USA.
                  www.DrRuthtanyi.org

Cover design and Interior layout by: AJ Design

Additional copies of this book can be obtained from:
                Online: www.DrRuthtanyi.org
                Email: Info@DrRuthtanyi.org

All Scripture quotations, unless otherwise indicated, are taken from the *Holy Bible, New International Version®, NIV®.* Copyright ©1973, 1978, 1984, 2011 by Biblica, Inc.™ Used by permission of Zondervan. All rights reserved worldwide.

Scripture quotations marked NLT are taken from the Holy Bible, New Living Translation, copyright ©1996, 2004, 2007, 2013, 2015 by Tyndale House Foundation. Used by permission of Tyndale House Publishers, Inc., Carol Stream, Illinois 60188. All rights reserved.

Scriptures marked NKJV are taken from the NEW KING JAMES VERSION (NKJV): Scripture taken from the NEW KING JAMES VERSION®. Copyright© 1982 by Thomas Nelson, Inc. Used by permission. All rights reserved.

Scriptures marked AMP are taken from the AMPLIFIED BIBLE (AMP): Scripture taken from the AMPLIFIED® BIBLE, Copyright © 1954, 1958, 1962, 1964, 1965, 1987 by the Lockman Foundation Used by Permission.

We want to hear from you. Please send your comments and/or testimonies about this book to: Info@DrRuthTanyi.org or write to:

       Dr. Ruth Tanyi Ministries, Inc
       P O BOX 1806
       Loma Linda, CA, 92354, USA.

If you find any error in the citation of Scripture anywhere in this book, kindly contact us so we can make the necessary corrections, thank you.

ISBN 978-0-9986689-2-5
Library of Congress Control Number: 2017918975

All rights Reserved. No part of this book may be reproduced in any form without written permission from Dr. Ruth Tanyi Ministries Inc.
Printed in the Unites States of America.

CONTENTS

Preface: Is the Bible Trustworthy?... 6

Introduction 8

Chapter 1: God's Story... 13

Chapter 2: Evidence # 1: Archeological Evidence 23

Chapter 3: Evidence # 2: Biblical Miracles 31

Chapter 4: Evidence # 3: Biblical Prophecies................................ 37

Chapter 5: Evidence # 4: Biblical Testimonies 47

Chapter 6: Evidence # 5: Honesty of Scripture 53

Chapter 7: Evidence # 6: Number of Biblical Manuscripts........... 61

Chapter 8: Evidence # 7: Consistency of Scripture 69

Chapter 9: Evidence # 8: Extra Biblical Writings.......................... 75

Chapter 10: Evidence # 9: Scientific Accuracy 81

Chapter 11: Evidence # 10: The Resurrection of Jesus Christ......... 87

Chapter 12: Be a Doer of the Word... 93

Concluding Remarks: It Will Change Your Life........................... 107

Bibliography 112

Ministry Resources 115

About the Author 119

DEDICATION

This book is dedicated to you, the reader, who is still "on the fence", and/or have never read the Bible. I am very glad that you are interested in knowing more about God's Word: the Bible, which is His Only inspired, infallible and inerrant Word to you. I pray for God to open your physical and spiritual eyes, so that you will come to a deeper revelation that His Words, as encased in the Bible, is **The Only Truth** that will equip you to live the life He created you to enjoy in the first place. By faith, I believe God will answer this prayer, in Jesus name, AMEN.

PREFACE

Is The Bible Trustworthy?

In my opinion, this is the most crucial question any true Christian should ask, and be 100% certain of the answer in order to peacefully practice Christianity. God has already revealed Himself to us through the person of Jesus Christ (Hebrews 1: 1-3), and has spoken to us through His written Word (2 Peter 1:19). Since that is the case, the Word of God encased in the Bible is the best and direct way to know God's heart, His will, and to walk with Him in this life. ***Although God can still speak to us through others, visions, dreams, situations/circumstances, and through any other means He sees fitting, the Bible remains the primary and the best way God speaks.***

The Apostle Peter had spent about 3 years with God Himself in the flesh: Jesus Christ; he was a firsthand eye witness of the miracles of Christ, and the transfiguration (Matthew 17:1-13). But, in spite of his eye witness account of God's majesty, the apostle clearly reiterated that the written Word of God is superior than visions or even the audible voice of God (see 2 Peter chapter 1); because your enemy, Satan, can manifest in the spiritual realm in the form of a vision, or a dream, etc, and deceive you (2 Corinthians 11:13-14). But if you know the Word of God, it will be difficult for Satan to deceive you. Since this is the case, it goes without saying that having an unshakable assurance about the validity of the Bible is absolutely essential.

As you are about to find out in this book, there is more evidence for the trustworthiness of the Bible than any other religious book in the history of the world. Anyone who is unbiased and studies the body of evidence I am about to present would have a very difficult time ignoring or dismissing them. **These evidences are not fictional, they are factual. There is a popular saying that "facts do not lie," although the interpretation of the facts might be slightly different. To this end, I hereby present the facts about the trustworthiness of the Bible without my interpretation, in order for you to evaluate the evidence for yourself.** I present these in no particular order of importance; they are all equally important. Lastly, because Christianity is a faith embedded in history, which can be verified and studied in real time and space, the body of evidence presented in this book is discussed in the context of world history.

October, 2017

Introduction

With all the different world religions claiming that their Scripture is inspired by some god, what makes the true Christian Bible different, some of you may wonder? Firstly, I want to clarify that true Christianity is not a religion; rather, it is a faith based relationship with The Only True living God of the heavens and the earth, the God of the true Christian Bible, through a personal relationship with His Son, Jesus Christ. Secondly, I used the phraseologies "true Christianity or" " true Christian" because there are pseudo Christian Man-made religious groups, such as the Jehovah's Witnesses and the Mormons, who claim to be Christians, but upon a closer study of their beliefs, it will be very obvious that they reject the true claims of Jesus Christ, especially His Deity. Thus, their own teachings and beliefs disqualify them as true followers of the Lord Jesus Christ.

So, while countless Scriptures from all Man-made religions exist, in addition to the Scriptures from pseudo-Christian cults (i.e., groups that deviate from the true teachings of the true Christian Bible), it is absolutely relevant to evaluate the evidence as to why the true Christian Bible is the Only inspired Holy Scriptures, from the Only True God of the heavens and the earth. **It is noteworthy to keep in mind that all of the Scriptures from all of the various world religions, including those of the various cults cannot all be true at the same time: Only one is true, period!** You know why? Because the Principle of Contradiction in classical logic teaches us that two mutually exclusive positions or statements cannot both be true at the same time; one is definitely false. Simplistically stated, what this means is that, the true Christian Bible and all of the various Scriptures from the various world religions cannot be true and/or inspired at the same time, especially because each of them is espousing different and/or contradictory doctrines (teachings) — you get the point?

With the aforementioned thought, the purpose of this book is to provide the body of evidence, and thus answer the question: *Can the true Christian Bible be trusted as The Only inspired Holy Scripture?* In doing so, it is my hope that, you, the reader, will come to a firm grasp that the inspired Words encased in the Bible, are indeed God's specific Words to you. Having this unshakeable knowing is essential in your journey as a Christian, because the primary way God speaks to us, His children, is through His written Words encased in the Bible.

Most importantly, everything we need as Christians in order to live a successful fruitful life on this earth has already been revealed to us in God's Word, the Bible. Thus, it is my prayer that this book will help you to approach the Bible, with much confidence, as inspired by God, thereby enabling you to easily obey God's decrees, which will in turn position you to receive His abundant blessings and provisions in this present life.

Much more, for those of you who are unsure about the trustworthiness of the Bible, it is also my prayer that, upon completing your study of this book, your faith will be quickened, and you will be emboldened, to confidently defend the claims of the Bible and your faith in Jesus Christ.

Additionally, for those of you who have never read the Bible and/or, are not acquainted with its teachings, I believe that this book will inspire and challenge you to start studying the Bible. And I guarantee you, based on the inspired, infallible (i.e., flawless) and inerrant (i.e., without error) Holy Scripture, if you are genuinely studying the Bible in order to know the true living God who inspired it, He will definitely speak to your heart through His Word, and you will be inspired, because the Bible is, indeed, inspired by God. Besides being inspired, if you truthfully study the Bible because you want a relationship with God, He will reveal more of Himself to you, through His Word.

Lastly, for the Christian and non-Christian alike reading this book, I pray that the body of evidence discussed herein, will solidify your trust and love for God, draw you closer to Him, and embolden you to share your faith with others. I pray all these in the name of Jesus Christ, AMEN!

October 2017

Other Teaching Materials by Dr Tanyi to help you Grow with God through Christ

BOOKS BY DR TANYI:

- *Are You Moving Forward with Jesus? / How to Excel In Your Identity in Christ.*
- *Answers to the Toughest 25 Questions about the Real Jesus.*
- *Can I trust the Bible as God's Word? How do I Know? What Is the Evidence?*
- *Faith to Receive God's Promises. How to "Walk" in Biblical Faith and Allow the Blessings of God to Chase You.*

COMING SOON!

- *13 Reasons Why People Get Sick! A Biblical Perspective & Remedies.*
- *Did God Really Say that? How to Overcome Doubt and Receive God's Promises: 10 Life-Changing Lessons Learned from Overcoming Metastasis Colon Cancer.*
- *A True Story of God's Unconditional Grace and Love: Healed by the Stripes of Jesus: My Story! My Miracle! How I Overcame Metastasis Colon Cancer.*

AUDIO CD TEACHING LIBRARY:

- *The Heart of True Christianity: The Gospel Message of Jesus Christ: Answers to 10 Major Questions Pertaining to Your Salvation in Christ Jesus.*
- *What Are the Gifts of the Spirit?*
- *Holy Spirit-Led Healthy Emotions: The Fruit of the Spirit and Your Health.*
- *How to Overcome Doubt and Receive God's Promises.*
- *13 Reasons Why People Get Sick: A Biblical Perspective & Remedies.*
- *Unforgiveness and Other Toxic Emotions: How to Walk in Forgiveness.*
- *Live Above Your Fears & Overcome Sicknesses and Diseases.*
- *Be Anxious No More.*
- *Daily Habits For Your Soul.*
- *Faith to Receive God's Promises / How to "Walk" in Biblical Faith and Allow the Blessings of God to Chase You.*
- *Are You Moving Forward with Jesus? / How to Excel In Your Identity in Christ.*

Grow in the Word of God and Receive His blessings through our Discipleship Bible Teaching Series.

The **Audio Podcast Series**, titled *"Biblical Principles for a Blessed Life,"* is an in-depth teaching through the entire Bible, from Genesis to the book of Revelation, focusing on major biblical principles, and teaching you how to apply those principles daily and receive God's blessings.

Biblical Preventive Health with Dr Ruth®
Biblical Preventive Health with Dr Ruth® is an educational magazine, which will educate individuals on how to integrate Bible-based principles into their lives, thereby preventing and overcoming sicknesses and diseases. You have heard what Medicine has to say! But do you know what the Bible says about a host of diseases plaguing people today? This magazine will teach you how to view your health from a godly perspective, and it offers practical recommendations to take care of God's temple.

13 Reasons Why True Christianity is Different: A Wall Mount Poster
This wall mount poster answers the question many individuals often ask: What makes Christianity different? This evangelistic poster will remind you daily of your unique relationship with God through Christ, and provide answers to confidently educate others and defend your faith. You will never be dumbfounded when asked to explain why your faith in Christ is unique, compared to other religions.

Obtaining Ministry Resources
To obtain additional copies of this book, or to get more information about the above ministry resources, please visit our Website:

www.DrRuthTanyi.org. You can also email, write or call us:

Dr. Ruth Tanyi Ministries, Inc
P O BOX 1806 I Loma Linda, CA, 92354, USA.
Email: Info@DrRuthtanyi.org
Phone: (909) 383-7978

CHAPTER 1

God's Story

Before I delve into much discussion about the body of evidence for the trustworthiness of the Bible, some basic introduction about the Bible is necessary. I present the data below in a very succinct manner, just to give you a general overview about God's story as recorded in the pages of the Bible.

The True Christian Bible

The true Christian Bible is the divinely written Word of God, a collection of 66 books, 39 Old Testament and 27 New Testament books, and accepted by the three branches of true Christianity: The Orthodox, Roman Catholics and Protestants, as the inspired Word of God. By inspired, I mean, God spoke His thoughts through various people, such as His prophets (i.e., a person who speaks utterances from God), across different generations, who wrote everything down as instructed by God (2 Peter 1:21). The three branches of true Christianity consider the Bible as the infallible (i.e., flawless) and inerrant (i.e., without error) Word of God, and the primary authority for the teachings of Christian doctrines (2 Timothy 3:16).

The Bible was written by about 40 different authors, over a period of about 1,500 (one thousand five hundred) years, across different generations and languages, yet consistent and unified in its theme: The revelation of God the Father, God the Son, and God the Holy Spirit, and God's story about His redemption of Mankind, since the transgression (i.e., willful disobedience) of Adam and Eve, as recorded in Genesis chapter 3.

God revealed Himself to us in the Bible as The Creator of the heavens and the earth (Genesis 1: 27-28). He created a perfect universe as recorded in Genesis chapters 1 and 2, and He said everything was good. Then, He created the first human beings, Adam and Eve, as tripartite beings, consisting of a mind, body and a spirit, and gave them dominion to rule over the earth (Genesis 1: 28), including caring for the Garden of Eden, which He had created. He also gave them a Free Will (i.e., the ability to make independent decisions), and instructed them not to eat from a particular tree in the Garden of Eden. But Adam and Eve were deceived by Satan, and they disobeyed God and ate from the forbidden tree.

Ever since that transgression, the Bible teaches that sin and death entered into God's perfect creation, and Mankind "fell from grace" (Romans 5:12). Since God is perfectly holy, sin separated Mankind (Adam and Eve) from fellowship with The Holy God, and Mankind's spirit, became darkened and dead, without access to God. Since All human beings can be traced back to a common ancestor Adam and Eve, every human being born into this world, inherits a Sinful Nature, due to that sin committed by Adam and Eve. And also, an individual with a darkened spirit cannot fellowship with The Holy God. God is love, in His very essence. Thus, in His love and desire to fellowship with His creation, Mankind, He came up with a plan to redeem Mankind from that "fallen state" in order to restore fellowship with His creation, us (Genesis 3:15).

God's Unconditional Love For Us

The entire Bible, from the book of Genesis to the book of Revelation, is the unfolding story of God's unconditional love, and His deepest quest to redeem His creation Mankind, from that "fallen state," after Adam and Eve were deceived by Satan. Although Adam failed due to disobedience, which led to sin and death, one person, Jesus Christ, succeeded. The Bible teaches us how the obedience of Jesus Christ has given Mankind life again, if we choose to accept God's free gift to us: The Lord Jesus. Under the inspiration of the Holy Spirit, the apostle Paul wrote in Romans chapter 5:

Therefore, just as sin entered the world through one man, and death through sin, and in this way death came to all people, because all sinned... For if the many died by the trespass of the one man, how much more did God's grace and the gift that came by the grace of the one man, Jesus Christ, overflow to the many!... just as sin reigned in death, so also grace might reign through righteousness to bring eternal life through Jesus Christ our Lord (vv. 12-21), (emphasis author's).

Since Christ is the central person in the true Christian faith, whatever He believes in, and/or teaches in the Bible is 100% considered Holy Scripture. As explained in the introduction section of this book, it is necessary to use the phraseology "true Christian" and/or "true Christianity" in order to distinguish it from pseudo Christian cults, such as the Jehovah's Witnesses and the Mormons who deny the claims of Jesus Christ as God Himself in the flesh. And according to Jesus Christ Himself, anyone who rejects Him, rejects God the Father (Luke 10:16; 1 John 2:23).

So anyone, or even any so called Christian groups that reject the claims of Jesus, including His claim as God, are not His true followers. Thus, moving forward in this book, I will use the phraseologies "true Christian (s)" and Christian interchangeably, to refer to those who have accepted All of the claims of Jesus Christ as found in the Bible, including His claim as God, and thus have a relationship with God the Father, and are indwelt by the Holy Spirit. Also, I will use the phraseologies "true Christian Bible" and/or the Bible interchangeably to refer to The Only inspired Holy Scriptures.

JESUS CHRIST: THE CENTER OF GOD'S STORY

Jesus Christ is central to God's story in the Bible. He is The promised Redeemer referred to in Genesis 3:15 (right after the transgression by Adam and Eve), who would overcome Satan and reconcile Mankind into fellowship with God again. All of the Old Testament Laws, sacrificial system, and the prophecies all pointed to Christ, the Messianic Redeemer of the world.

Jesus Christ was/is God Himself in the flesh, meaning, in the form of a human being. He experienced a divine birth, as His mother, Mary, was supernaturally pregnant by the Holy Spirit and gave birth to Him. Jesus Christ had two distinct natures: He was 100% God; and 100% a human being, like one of us.

The Bible teaches us that Jesus Christ was the eternal Word of God that supernaturally became a human being (John 1:1-14). Jesus Christ lived a sinless life (1 Peter 2:22), and fulfilled All of the Old Testament Messianic prophecies 100% (Luke 24:25–27; Galatians 4:4-5). The Lord Jesus also taught His followers how to live in accordance with the Word of God practically and purposefully. As a human being, He relied on the Word of God to overcome Satan (Matthew 4:1-11). He frequently quoted out of the Old Testament, and reminded others about Himself in the Old Testament Scriptures (John 5:46-47).

Christ Jesus unequivocally taught that the living Word of God found in the Bible is the Only source of life (John 6:63). He also taught on the permanency of the Word of God (Matthew 24:35), and clearly warned that only those who actually practice the Word of God are His true followers and would yield much results as God's children on this earth (Luke 6:46-49).

> *Most importantly, the Lord taught that He will judge each one of us, in the last day, in accordance with the Word of God (John 12:48). Thus, the Word of God is the only standard for evaluation and judgment in regards to ALL things pertaining to God, in this life and in eternity.*

The Bible: Real Stories and Real Events in History

In telling God's story, the Bible contains stories of real people who existed, with real stories and events, which happened in history. The Bible documented real issues human beings encountered, and continue to experience as a result of disobedience and sin, such as, but not limited to, fear, worry, anxiety, jealousy, murder, lying, thievery, etc, etc. Also, other human issues pertaining to loneliness, love, conflict resolution, financial stewardship, family life, raising children, friendships, etc, are all recorded in the pages of the Bible. In dealing with the full range of human experiences and emotions, God, in His love, has provided the solutions and/or remedies as written in the Bible, for how His children should live in this life and overcome, if they chose to obey Him.

The Bible, which is historical, contains different types of literature, such as narratives (e.g., the book of Genesis); poetry (the book of Psalms); prophecies (e.g., the book of Isaiah); wisdom literature (e.g., the book of Proverbs); apocalyptic (the book of Revelation); the Gospels (the Ministry of Jesus Christ); epistles or letters (e.g., 1 and 2 Corinthians); etc.

God has already spoken, and the Bible is canonized, meaning, all 66 books of the Bible are the only inspired books by God, accepted by the body of Christ (i.e., a collection of all true Christians across the world, regardless of denominational preference), to be used as **The** guide for true Christian doctrines for leading and guiding Christians (2 Timothy 3:16). The Bible teaches us that God spoke through the prophets during the Old Testament era, but now, God has fully revealed Himself in the person of Jesus Christ (Hebrews 1:1-2). Therefore, everything we need as Christians to live successfully has already been provided to us by God in His Word, we need not look elsewhere.

THE BIBLE: GOD'S IMMUTABLE TIMELESS TRUTHS ACROSS ALL GENERATIONS AND CENTURIES

God's Words found in the Bible are immutable (i.e., unchangeable), flawless (Proverbs 30:5), and inerrant (i.e., without error).

> *While the Bible was written thousands of years ago, the Truths found in its pages are timeless, and are still relevant to us today, just like it was thousands of year ago at the time it was written. The Bible is not "just a book", like some people view it. Rather, it is The book of life, and the Words found in its pages are The only source of life*
> *(John 6:63).*

There has never been, and there will never be a book like the Bible. It is the number one bestselling book in every generation and in every Century. The Bible has transformed millions of lives, for the better, across every generation; it has transformed pagan cultures and civilizations into God fearing nations; it has transformed governments, and inspired many moral laws that govern countless nations today. The Bible is the only book that has been translated into over 1000 (one thousand) languages of the world, and it continues to transform lives across the globe, daily.

Additionally, the absolute Truths found in the Bible have set millions of people free from all sorts of physical, emotional and spiritual bondages. It has "saved" countless marriages worldwide from the devastating effects of divorce and separation. The best hospitals, universities, and other charitable organizations that have helped countless of people across every generation have been founded and governed based on biblical principles.

Because the timeless Truths found in the Bible are God's Words to His creation: Mankind, they have the same effect across different age groups, cultures, and gender worldwide. The Truths in the Bible will work equally for everyone who practice them faithfully, regardless of geographical location, because God is no respecter of persons — He will honor and reward His Word and obedience, period! The timeless truths in the Bible will teach you how to raise godly children, manage your finances, relationships, conflicts, etc, etc. The Bible has All of the answers to life's biggest problems.

Much more, the Bible offers the Only source of true hope in this world; Its timeless teachings are the main source for strength, joy, hope, assurance, protection, deliverances, etc, to millions of individuals daily across the world. Most significantly, the Bible provides you with the answers to the fundamental questions about your existence: (1) who you are? ; (2) why you are here on the earth?; (3) what your specific purpose for life is?; (4) what your final destination will be after you die? The answers to these questions are all found in the pages of the Bible.

God, Who created Mankind anticipated the kinds of problems we will encounter in this life, and thus provided the solutions to us, in His Word. God created us in His image (Genesis 1:27-28). Hence, at the core, all human beings are the same, although we may appear different on the outside. This means that, all of us, human beings, experience the same physical, emotional and spiritual issues and/or problems, regardless of where we live on the earth, which explains why the Bible speaks to the hearts of Mankind across every generation, culture, race, ethnicity, gender, government, etc.

And, keep this absolute Truth in mind: the Word of God is eternal, and has always existed, even before God created the earth (Psalm 119:89). **<u>Thus, while the Word of God is written by Men, it is not from Men, but from God</u>**. **Therefore, whatever the Bible says, it is indeed God who says it! Hence, the popular saying: "If the Bible says it, I believe it, and that settles it". Better yet, I like to restate this saying like this: "If the Bible says it, God says it, and that settles it"! So true, in Jesus name, AMEN!**

SUMMARY POINTS:

- Because of God's unconditional love for us, He became a human being in the person of Jesus Christ, in order to redeem us from our Sinful Nature;
- The timeless Truths found in the Bible are immutable, and applicable to us today, right now, just like it did to our fellow human beings at the time the Bible was written;
- God will always honor and reward obedience to His Word, regardless of our geographical location, culture, or gender, etc;
- The Bible is the Only inspired and inerrant Word of God, which has transformed millions of individuals, civilizations, governments, in every generation and Century;
- When it is all "said and done", at the final judgment, God will judge each of us based on the teachings found in His Word;
- The flawless Word of God is eternal.

POINTS FOR CONSIDERATION:

- What are your thoughts about the fact that the 40 different authors who wrote the Bible lived Centuries apart in different areas of the world, yet, they were all telling the same story? Do you think it is a coincidence?
- Have you ever pondered on the notion that when it is all "said and done", you will be judged in accordance with the decrees in God's Word?

CHAPTER 2

EVIDENCE #1:

ARCHEOLOGICAL EVIDENCE

In this chapter, through chapter 11 of this book, I will begin to answer the major question of why the Bible can be trusted as God's inspired, infallible, and inerrant Word. Because of the exceedingly overwhelming body of evidence to support the trustworthiness of the Bible, I am unable to expound on all of these evidences in this book, primarily, due to space limitation. Nonetheless, I will be selective, as I expound, in a very succinct manner, on 10 major reasons why you can trust the Bible. I begin with archeological evidence.

Archeology is a science that studies how people lived in the past, including their culture, environment, etc. Most of the time this information is buried in the ground. As such, Archeologists would then dig up the data to study and learn more about the people's past and their culture. Some of you may be wondering about the significance of archeological evidence? Archeological evidence is important to validate the Bible's stories because the Bible is a historical book written in the context of history with names, places and events than can either validate or disprove it. However, **there is one thing archeological evidence cannot do — it cannot** *prove that the Bible is inspired.* Nonetheless, archeological evidence can verify events, nations, places, and names discussed in the Bible.

To date, over 25,000 (twenty five thousand) archeological discoveries have been made to support biblical data, and I am certain that by the time of this publication, more discoveries would have been made. Given that the archeological discoveries are overwhelming, I am unable to discuss most of them here; thus, I will be selective in my discussion of just a few from the Old and New Testaments. Those of you interested in an in-depth study of this topic can consult the bibliography list at the end of this book for further study.

Discoveries Supporting the Old Testament

There are many critics of the Bible who have espoused that the stories in the Old Testament are outright fictional. Well, God has proved them as liars, because thousands of evidences over the last hundreds of years have proved that the critics and doubters have been wrong all along. Below are some of these evidences:

1. Throughout all of the continents of the world, fossil records (i.e., accumulation of remains of organisms mostly in sedimentary rocks or other geologic deposits) of billions of dead animals and plants have been found buried under sedimentary rocks. According to archeologists, paleontologists (i.e., researchers who study fossil records about the past), geologists (i.e., researchers who study the earth), the manner in which the billions of animals and other creatures were preserved when discovered are all consistent, and suggestive of a massive flood. This is so because the creatures were rapidly buried in the mud, consistent with the massive flood as described in the book of Genesis;

2. Evidence of the collapsed walls of the city of Jericho as described in the Bible has been found;

3. Evidence of the settlement of the Israelites in Egypt as discussed in Genesis 42 through 47 has been found;

4. Evidence of the existence of King David as mentioned in first and second Samuel, has been discovered;

5. Evidence of the Philistines as discussed in the Bible, has been discovered;

6. Evidence of the Hittites as discussed in the Bible, has been found near modern day Turkey;

7. The city of Nineveh, as discussed in the Bible, in the book of Jonah, was unearthed in 1847;

8. The palace of Sargon, King of Assyria, as described in Isaiah 20:1, has been found;

9. The Dead Sea Scrolls were found in 1947, which included entire books of almost every copy of the Old Testament, dating as far back as approximately the third Century. These scrolls were found to be identical to our contemporary copies of the Old Testament, proving that the Bible we have today is absolutely accurate and reliable as passed down to us from the original authors. This discovery of the Dead Sea Scrolls also lend credibility and confidence in the translation process from the original languages of the Bible to English; we can indeed trust the Bible.

DISCOVERIES SUPPORTING THE NEW TESTAMENT

Like the Old Testament, hundreds of discoveries pertaining to people, events and places discussed throughout the New Testament in the Bible have been unearthed. Below are just a few of such evidences.

1. Jacob's Well, as described in John 4:1-6, has been found;

2. The Pool of Bethesda, as described in John chapter 5, has been discovered;

3. The Pool of Siloam, as described in John chapter 9, has been unearthed;

4. The burial site of the High Priest, Caiaphas, who played a major role in the sentencing of our Lord Jesus, as described in the Gospel accounts has been revealed;

5. The city of Capernaum, where our Lord Jesus Christ lived for sometime as discussed in the Gospel accounts, has been found;

6. Inscriptions with the name of Pontius Pilate, the Roman governor, who washed his hands off of the innocent blood of the Lord Jesus as described in the Gospel accounts in the Bible, has been discovered;

7. The story described in Acts chapter 12 about the death of Herod Agrippa has been verified and written by historian Flavius Josephus, in Josephus *Antiquities,* and evidences of Herod's Palace have been found;

8. Biblical critics used to contend that the practice of crucifixion with nails was not practiced by the Romans, and as such they were implying that the death of Jesus by crucifixion was a hoax. These critics have been disgraced, as today, there is a plethora of archeological evidence verifying that crucifixion was a common practice by the Romans. In his writings, historian Flavius Josephus wrote

Evidence #1: Archeological Evidence

extensively about thousands of people crucified by the Romans; he also wrote about the crucifixion of Jesus Christ;

9. Archeological evidence is consistent with the fact that the early Christians worshipped Jesus Christ as God;

10. Numerous evidences of places and names mentioned in the book of Luke in the Bible, have been discovered;

11. There is a plethora of evidence showing that the writings of the early Church Fathers in the first three Centuries are consistent with the Bible we have today, thus validating the accuracy of our contemporary Bibles.

I could go on and on with archeological evidence to prove the validity of the Bible, but that is not necessary as I am sure by now you get the point.

Archeological evidence has added much confidence in the historicity of the Bible, and amplifies the accuracy and reliability of the inspired stories told, by providing external evidence for the authenticity of the Bible. Conversely, to date, no other Religious Book, in the history of the world, that claim to be inspired, such as those belonging to Mormons, Jehovah's Witnesses or Muslims (i.e., the Koran) has tenable archeological evidence in existence to support their claims.

Only the Bible has such verifiable evidence to support its claims. As such, the Bible has set the precedence for other so called inspired books to prove any existing archeological evidence to support the names, places and stories described in their pages: *None of them do, except the Bible, so trust it. It is the only inspired book from the One True God.*

SUMMARY POINTS:

- Archeological evidence does not prove that the Bible is inspired by God, but they add credibility and validity in regards to the accuracy of biblical events, places and accounts of things; countless archeological evidence across different Centuries support biblical claims;
- There are more archeological evidence supporting the claims of the true Christian Bible, compared to other so-called religious books of the world which have no verifiable archeological evidence to support their claims;
- The Bible can be trusted as the only inspired and inerrant Word of God.

POINTS FOR CONSIDERATION:

- What do you think about the fact that no other so called religious book in the history of the world has such verifiable, consistent, and validated archeological evidence to support its claims? Do you think the biblical evidence is a coincidence?
- What do archeological discoveries tell you about God's story?

CHAPTER 3

Evidence #2: Biblical Miracles

The word miracle is overused today to mean anything from finding a parking spot on a Super Bowl Sunday, to finding a spouse, to overcoming addictions, or avoiding traffic delays (if you live in Southern California), etc. But in its truest sense, none of the above, or the multitudes of ways we use this word denotes what a true miracle really is.

So what then is a miracle? According to the American Heritage Dictionary, a miracle is defined as " *An event that happens inexplicable by the laws of nature and so is held to be supernatural in origin or an act of God."* A miracle is further described as a spontaneous event that comes on its own without being summoned.

Then according to the Vine's Complete Expository Dictionary of Old and New Testament Words, a miracle is defined as *"power, inherent ability," describing works of supernatural origin and character that could not be produced by natural means or agents; it is a sign of divine authority."* As you can see, miracles require divine intervention, as they supersede nature, therefore it becomes supernatural. By implication therefore, a miracle requires some kind of evidence, "sign," or proof to validate its occurrence.

WHAT IS THE BIBLICAL EVIDENCE FOR MIRACLES?

The Bible is replete with the supernatural. Throughout the Old and New Testaments, God confirmed His Words through the Old Testament prophets with multiple miracles. For example, Moses parted the Red Sea (see Exodus chapter 14); Elijah called down fire from heaven (see I Kings chapter 18); Joshua stilled the Sun and the Moon (see Joshua chapter 10); Elijah was raptured (i.e., taken from earth straight into heaven without dying), (see 2 Kings); etc.

In the New Testament, the birth of Jesus Christ alone is beyond human reasoning, it was a miracle (see the Gospels). Much more, the miracles of the Lord Jesus alone, as described in the Gospel account in the New Testament can be grouped into three areas, all pointing to the supernatural nature of the Bible : These categories are: (1) *Healings*: Jesus Christ healed the blind; the crippled; the paralyzed; the deaf, etc; (2) **The Lord Jesus'** *authority over nature*: Jesus walked on water; supernaturally fed the multitudes; calmed the storm; spoke a Word and withered the fig tree; obtained money from the fish's mouth, etc; (3) *Raising the Dead*: Jesus Christ raised Lazarus, the widow of Nain's son, Jairus's daughter from the dead. And the climactic moment of all is that God the Father, raised Him, Jesus Christ , from the dead (see the Gospels).

In the New Testament, Jesus' followers, the apostles, healed the sick and raised the dead. The apostles performed multiple other miracles, such as when Peter walked on water (see the Gospels; the book of Acts). I could go on and on about miracles, but suffice it to say that, no other religious book, such as the books of Mormon, Jehovah's Witnesses, the Koran or the Sacred writings of Chinese Religions, Buddhism or Hinduism have been supernaturally confirmed by the God of the Bible, the Only True living God, through miracles: except the Bible!

Evidence #2: Biblical Miracles

Because the God of the Bible is **The** supernatural God of the heavens and the earth, miracles are one major way He reveals Himself. As such, He has confirmed the work of His prophets in the Old testament, and His apostles in the New Testament through verifiable miracles, authenticated by credible eye witnesses. The miracles of the Bible occurred in such a manner that they were verifiable by credible eye witnesses who risked their lives to testify (e.g., see John Chapter 9).

Conversely, the works, writings or sayings of other religious leaders such as Muhammad (Islam Religion); Joseph Smith (Mormonism) ; Confucius (Chinese Religion); or various writings from Buddhism, Hinduism or Jehovah's Witnesses have never been confirmed by the One True God, the God of the Bible, through miracles nor verified by credible eye witnesses.

Some of you may be surprised to know that the claims of other religions of the world, and even those of pseudo-Christian religions such as Mormonism and Jehovah's Witnesses, have not been "backed up" by the presence of God through His miracles. You know why? Because true Christianity is the only true faith in existence today and forevermore, and is exceedingly embedded in supernatural events that are verifiable, because there is Only One God, the God of the true Christian Bible.

Today, in the 21st Century, the God of the Bible continues to display His miracles through His faithful workers. In the body of Christ, which is a collection of all true Christians globally, all kinds of miracles, such as, but not limited to, people being healed from incurable and/or terminal diseases, others being raised from the dead, deafness and blindness being cured, etc, continue to abound.

I am aware that there are many individuals who do not believe in miracles. To this, I simply say: Your opinion does not change the fact that God exists, and He created this entire universe that you can physically see right now; so, miracles are happening every day. You might as well "wake up" and stop denying the obvious. Besides, your very existence is a miracle from God, who created you in His very image (Genesis 1:27-28).

The God of the Bible has, and continues to use miracles as a way to speak to us, His creation! Thus, miracles are real, and the Bible is a book of miracles, because we serve a supernatural, miraculous God, who has revealed Himself fully, in His inspired Word, the true Christian Bible. You can totally trust the Bible as God's Word to you.

SUMMARY POINTS:

- Only the Bible has verifiable, corroborated eye witness accounts of miracles from God;
- The miracles of Jesus Christ confirm 100%, that the Bible is the only inspired book, by the only God of the heavens and the earth: The God of the Bible;
- Other so-called religious books of the world have no verifiable or corroborated evidence of miracles from the Only true God of the heavens and the earth.

POINTS FOR CONSIDERATION:

- What are your thoughts about the fact that no other so-called world religion can back up their claims with verifiable, eye witness, authenticated evidence of true miracles?
- What do you think about the fact that the only true God, the God of the Bible, has not revealed Himself in the other world religions through verifiable miracles?

CAN I TRUST THE BIBLE AS GOD'S WORD?

CHAPTER 4

EVIDENCE #3:

BIBLICAL PROPHECIES

The word prophecy is one of those words in the English language that in my opinion, is loosely used by many today, including counterfeits, such as "psychics". The Vine's Dictionary of Old and New Testament Words defines prophecy as " *the speaking forth of the mind and counsel of God."* It is declaring something that cannot be known by natural means— it is the foretelling of God's will regarding the past, present or future.

The God of the Bible takes this matter of prophecy so seriously that in Deuteronomy 18:22, He has set standards for evaluating a false prophet based on prophecy: *"If what a prophet proclaims in the name of the Lord does not take place or come true, that is a message the Lord has not spoken. That prophet has spoken presumptuously, so do not be alarmed"* (emphasis author's). Yet, today, people still believe the multitude of so called "psychics" who claim to have supernatural abilities to predict the future, although their predictions are often vague, ambiguous, and guesses that are in line with the trends of the time, thus lending themselves to multiple possible outcomes.

With regards to false prophecies, I really like the way Norman Geisler noted that a study of prophecies from 1975 to 1981, including those of the popular psychic, Dixon, revealed that out of 72 of the predictions examined, only about 6 came to pass somewhat vaguely. And among those that came to pass, none was exact or precise; rather, they were mostly vague speculations that were consistent with the trend of the time, which could have been easily explained by chance, and having a general knowledge of worldly events and circumstances.

::

Conversely, biblical prophecies are extremely precise, clear, direct, repeated and are consistent; and biblical prophets have made absolutely no errors in their predictions, because they were inspired to speak from God.

::

WHAT IS THE SUPPORTING EVIDENCE FOR BIBLICAL PROPHECIES?

The Bible is a prophetic book, in which God has revealed hundred of prophecies, with over half of the prophecies, especially in the Old Testament, already fulfilled exactly as prophesied. For example:

1. God forewarned Noah about the flood, and it was precisely fulfilled (see the book of Genesis);

2. God promised Abraham he would have a son, Isaac, in his old age, it came to pass precisely (see the book of Genesis);

3. God forewarned Abram that his descendants (referring to the Jews) would be strangers in a foreign country, and they would be enslaved and mistreated for 400 years, it came to pass as prophesied (see the books of Genesis and Exodus);

4. God foretold Moses that he would deliver his people

Evidence #3: Biblical Prophecies

from Egyptian bondage, it was fulfilled exactly (see the book of Exodus);

5. God told Joshua that he would conquer his enemies and possess the Promised Land, it came to pass precisely (see the book of Joshua);

6. God told King Saul through Samuel that the Kingdom of Israel would be taken away from him, it came to pass exactly as predicted (see the book of 1 Samuel), etc.

The list is endless, but you get the point as this type of precision in predictions can only come from God. Additionally, in the New Testament, as an example:

i. Jesus prophesied that Peter would deny Him, it happened exactly as foretold;

ii. Jesus prophesied about the destruction of Jerusalem, it came to pass around 70 A.D.;

iii. Jesus prophesied about His death and resurrection, it happened precisely (see the Gospels);

iv. Jesus prophesied that His disciples would abandon Him once He was arrested, it came to pass perfectly, etc, etc.

In addition, in the case of the Lord Jesus being the Messiah, the exact place and time of His birth, the exact lineage, type of ministry and manner of His suffering, death and resurrection, were all precisely predicted about 400 years by the Old Testament Saints before He (Christ) was even born. This type of exactness is not humanly possible, especially because the old Testament Saints wrote and lived Centuries apart for the most part. Because the Bible is divinely inspired, God revealed this knowledge to His Saints through prophecy.

Because the Lord Jesus is the central person in the true Christian Bible, it is most relevant that we take a closer look at prophecies about Him. There are several hundreds, but space limitation prevents me from listing even up to 10% of the prophecies about Jesus Christ; I will only discuss a few here. Jesus Christ, the promised Messiah, and God's gift to Mankind, fulfilled hundreds of Old Testament prophecies as the Messiah, below are just a few examples.

A Few Old Testament Prophecies About the Messiah (Jesus Christ) and the New Testament Fulfillment

The Bible prophesied that the Messiah would:

Old Testament Prophecy	Old Testament Scripture	New Testament Fulfillment
Be born of a virgin	Isaiah 7:14	Matthew 1:23
Be a descendant of Isaac	Genesis 17:19	Luke 3:34
Be a descendant of Abraham	Genesis 12:3	Matthew 1:1
Also come from Egypt	Hosea 11:1	Matthew 2:14
Have a forerunner	Isaiah 40:3	Matthew 3:1
Be born in Bethlehem	Micah 5:2	Luke 2:4
Be from the tribe of Judah	Genesis 49:10	Luke 3:33
Be born the seed of a woman	Genesis 3:15	Galatians 4:4

Evidence #3: Biblical Prophecies

Old Testament Prophecy	Old Testament Scripture	New Testament Fulfillment
Be crucified and His hands and feet pierced	Psalm 22: 16	John 19: 18; Matthew 27:35
Suffer and die for the sins of the world	Isaiah 53: 4-5	Matthew 8: 14-17
Be betrayed for 30 pieces of Silver and the money cast on the Temple floor	Zechariah 11:12-13	Matthew 27:5-10
Be rejected by His own people (the Jews) and accepted by the Gentiles (Non Jews)	Psalm 118:22; Isaiah 49:6	Matthew 21:42
Be anointed and be eternal	Psalm 45:6-7	Hebrews 1: 8-12
Be born and His birth would trigger a slaughter of children	Jeremiah 31:15	Matthew 2:16-18
Be forsaken by God on the cross	Psalm 22:1	Matthew 27:45-46
Be offered sour wine for His thirst on the cross	Psalm 69:21	Matthew 27:34
Have His garments divided among the soldiers	Psalm 22:18	Matthew 27:35

Statistics is a scientific discipline that focuses on applying mathematical techniques in interpreting and analyzing data in order to reach a scientific conclusion. Over the years, statisticians have applied the principles of probability to scientifically investigate the probability of Jesus being the Messiah.

In their book, Science Speaks, Statisticians Peter Stoner and Robert Newman investigated the probability of *any one man in the world* at any given time fulfilling **just 8** of the Old Testament prophecies about Jesus. I have already mentioned how " facts do not lie," although the interpretation of the facts may be subjective and skewed.

Thus, to answer the question whether or not any one man that has ever lived in this life, beginning from the Old Testament era to this present time might have fulfilled just 8 of the Old Testament prophecies about Jesus, Stoner and Newman concluded that, the probability of any individual to have done so *is **1 in 10^{17}***. In writing this out, it will look like this: **100,000,000,000,000,000.**

Okay, if you do not like numbers, or if this does not make sense to you yet, Stoner and Newman described that it is like taking 10^{17} silver dollars and laying them across all of the city of Texas, which will actually cover the entire state, approximately two feet deep; then, place a certain mark on a particular silver dollar, and then mix up everything. Thereafter, blindfold a person, and tell him or her they can travel across Texas as many times as possible, but he or she must pick out that particular "marked" silver dollar among the rest. Boy, this would be impossible to do without God's intervention!

In the scenario just described above, what are the chances that the individual will select and/or find that particular "marked" silver dollar among all of them, while blindfolded? Likewise, the probability of that blindfolded individual finding

Evidence #3: Biblical Prophecies

that "marked" silver dollar (which is almost impossible without God's intervention), would be the same probability that the Old Testament prophets would have had in writing about Jesus Christ as the Messiah, with just 8 prophecies that all came to pass, if they prophesied without God's inspiration. Whao! A very strong argument showing how statistics points to Jesus Christ as the Messiah. You get the picture? In essence, it is almost, literally impossible, that these 8 prophecies studied by Stoner and Newman about the Lord Jesus alone are not true — Thus, they are all true, God spoke through the prophets.

Given the certainty that these prophecies came from The God of the Bible, Stoner and Newman added that the 8 prophecies they studied either came from God, or the prophets wrote them down based on their own human wisdom. Nonetheless, if the prophets used human wisdom, Stoner and Newman clarified that, they, referring to the prophets, would have only had 1 chance in 10^{17} that they would be fulfilled in one person: whao! The great news is that, the prophecies came true in Christ, exactly as prophesied. Thus, the fulfillment of just 8 prophecies means that God inspired the Old Testament prophets to write down these prophecies about Christ, which came to pass exactly as prophesied. You can indeed, trust the Bible as God's inspired Word!

For just a moment, think about a baby. If a baby can walk 20 feet, then that baby can certainty walk 10 feet, right? Absolutely! In the same way, if the chances (using statistical probability), of just 8 Old Testament prophecies about Jesus are right, then obviously the chances of the rest of them being right are???? (you fill in the blank). The bottom line is this: these prophecies could only have been fulfilled exactly as prophesied in the Old Testament because they were given by God Himself. No other religious book has such verifiable precise predictions that have come to pass: only the Bible has this!. The Bible can be trusted!

It is interesting how people take chances in their everyday life, and in their business dealings, including who to get married to, which house to buy, where to attend college, etc. But yet, when it comes to the Bible, people are willing to ignore this same logic, and reject Jesus Christ as the Messiah. Essentially, people are taking a chance with their eternity. But, keep in mind that you only have one chance, in this present life, to accept Jesus Christ as your personal Lord and Savior, or reject Him. Once you die, it will be too late. So "gamble" wisely, and accept Jesus Christ as your Savior, today.

Remember, numbers or **"facts do not lie**." You can choose to reject the prophecies and reject Christ, but that does not change the fact: He is the promised Messiah, and God Himself in the flesh as He claims, and, as stated in the Bible. I hope you do not reject this critical evidence and gamble with your eternity: Jesus loves you, and desires a relationship with you.

Most importantly, keep in mind that only the Bible has such precise prophecies about Jesus Christ, the promised Messiah, God Himself in the flesh. This alone is a critical evidence to validate All of the claims of the Bible, period!

SUMMARY POINTS:

- ❧ The Bible is a prophetic book, with exact prophecies that have come to pass, validating its authenticity as God's Inspired Word;
- ❧ Jesus Christ fulfilled All of the Messianic prophecies precisely, down to the tiniest detail;
- ❧ Biblical prophecies, which are 100% exact/precise, prove that the Bible is indeed God's inspired Word;
- ❧ No other so-called religious book in the history of the world has prophecies in their Scriptures, which have come to pass precisely, except the Bible

POINTS FOR CONSIDERATION:

- ❧ What do you think about the fact that "numbers do not lie"? Since All of the facts point to Jesus Christ as the Messiah prophesied throughout the Old Testament, isn't that sufficient to authenticate the validity of the Bible as God's only inspired Word? What do you think?
- ❧ What are your thoughts about the fact that the other world religions have no verifiable prophecies compared to true Christianity?

CHAPTER 5

Evidence #4: Biblical Testimonies

In today's world, the word testimony can mean different things to different people, but to true Christians, it often refers to the work of God in our lives. The Strong Concordance defines the word testimony as a *"witness borne in behalf of something."* In the Greek, the word *Marturion* is a noun, which is translated in English as "a testimony, witness." This testimony or witness borne on behalf of something is referring to God, a witness to the presence of God in a Christian's life. Although this is a subjective phenomenon, it is nonetheless powerful, as evidence for the trustworthiness of the Bible. Beside biblical testimonies, there are thousands of other Christians whose testimonies have transformed the lives of others, and have served as the main reason for so many others to become a follower of Jesus Christ.

I personally know of people who were "hard core" drug addicts and alcoholics, and when they became Christians and allowed God to work in their lives, they were able to quit the addiction "cold turkey" without any withdrawal symptoms, which is unheard of in any case of a true physiological addiction. Usually, a chronic substance addict would suffer from some kind of withdrawal due to the physiological dependence on the substance, but this has not been the case in the individuals I am referring to.

In my own life, being healed from metastasis colon cancer and various subsequent diseases brought on by the cancer is a testimony of God's presence and miracles in my life (I discuss more of this in another book). I know several others, such as my Pastor, Diego Mesa, who was healed from terminal kidney cancer, and many others who have been healed from incurable diseases, etc. There are thousands of other testimonies I could share, but I want to focus on biblical testimonies in this section in order to highlight the trustworthiness of the Bible. Specifically, I want to focus on the apostles in the New Testament, those individuals whom God used to initially advance Christianity worldwide, after the resurrection of our Lord Jesus from the dead and His ascension into heaven.

What is the Supporting Evidence For Biblical Testimonies?

For those of you who are not aware of the apostle Paul's conversion, a brief introduction would be helpful. The apostle Paul (previously called Saul) was a master persecutor of Christians before his conversion. In Acts 7:54-58, we are told how he was a witness to the stoning death of Stephen, a faithful follower of Jesus Christ. Then in Acts chapter 9, on his way to persecute and probably kill more Christians, the " Risen Christ," Himself, appeared to him. This appearance was so transforming that it led to Saul's conversion as a Christian, and he accepted God's calling in his life to be the apostle to the Gentiles (non-Jews). Thereafter, his name was changed from Saul to Paul.

The apostle Paul was extremely zealous about the Jewish Law, thus he was determined on persecuting the Church of Christ because in his "twisted mind", they were violating

God's Law. He believed sincerely, although he was grossly wrong, that he was doing the right thing on God's behalf (see Acts chapter 22). It is my opinion that had God, in the form of the "Risen Christ" not intervened directly, no amount of logic or reasoning would have converted the apostle Paul , who was highly educated in the Jewish Law. After his conversion and acceptance of God's calling in his life, he went on to transform Christianity and became the second most influential person in the history of Christianity after Jesus Christ. His conversion and testimony alone has convinced many people throughout world history, including some atheists, to become Christians, as only God, can work such a miracle in a person's life.

The apostle Paul's testimony of the presence of God in his life is evidenced in his ministry throughout the New Testament. He is responsible for writing over 50% of the New Testament. He was the first major missionary of the Church (i.e., the Universal Church, meaning, all of the various churches worldwide that are preaching and practicing true Christianity). He performed multiple miracles; and is credited as the person responsible for the initial spread of Christianity following the ascension of our Lord. The apostle himself later experienced major persecution in his ministry from the Jews and others, and thus suffered enormously; yet, he remained joyful, tenacious, and faithful to his calling and felt honored to be called by God.

The anointing and grace in the apostle Paul's life to endure the hardships during his ministry could have only come from God; his life was a true testimony of the presence of God. If it were not a true conversion from God, it is highly unlikely that the apostle Paul would have endured the horrific hardships he experienced and persevered throughout his ministry with gladness and encouragement to others. Church history noted that he was eventually martyred, and even to his death, he was joyful and appreciative to God for his ministry: Whao! He left an unprecedented example for all true Christians.

Without the presence of God in the apostle Paul's life, it would have been humanly impossible to accomplish what he did for the first Century Church. His testimony attest to the trustworthiness of the Bible:

God equips those He chooses for His Divine purposes, and displays His presence in their lives. No other individual, in any other religion of the world, has come close to accomplishing what the apostle Paul did for Christianity. You know why? Because the One True God of the Bible was his primary source of strength and companion.

The apostle Peter and the other disciples of the Lord Jesus are other excellent examples of biblical testimony to attest to the trustworthiness of the Bible. In the Gospel account, Peter confidently promised Jesus he would never deny him, but Peter later denied knowing the Lord. The Lord Jesus had also prophesied that His disciples would abandon Him, and indeed, they all ran away when He was arrested. In other instances throughout the Gospel account, the disciples came across as weak , fearful, quarrelsome men fighting over wanting the greatest position in Jesus' Kingdom, etc. But after the resurrection of Jesus, and after the disciples were filled with the Holy Spirit and endued with God's power, there was a dramatic transformation in their lives because of the presence of God's power.

The testimonies of the disciples as transformed men was like a " night and day" transformation that could only be attributed to God. These previously fearful and weak disciples became bold and fearless as they proclaimed the Gospel with unbelievable confidence and power, and performed multiple verifiable eye witness miracles. Their boldness and fearless spirits to proclaim the Gospel of Jesus Christ led to their deaths. With the exception of the apostle John, all of the disciples were killed for their faith according to Church history. And in spite of their impending death, none of them recanted or denounced their faith: those were true testimonies because of the presence of God in their lives. These types of testimonies are only unique to the Bible, no other religious book has such verifiable evidence of testimonies as those documented in the Bible.

For those of you still doubting these apostles' testimonies and transformations, the main thing to keep in mind is that, if a testimony is truly from God, it will sustain over time and pass the test of time.

And this was the case with the apostles — their testimonies stood the test of time, as God filled them daily with His Holy Spirit, and they grew bolder, displaying God's miracles in their respective lives and ministries (see the book of Acts in the Bible). All these happened because the supernatural miraculous God of the true Christian Bible manifested Himself in the lives of these apostles. No other religious book since the creation of the world can claim such testimonies about the individuals listed in their Scriptures, you know why? Because only the Bible is inspired by the Only True living God. Yes, you can trust the Bible as God's Word to you.

Summary Points:

- ༄ The conversion and transformation of the apostle Paul alone has been sufficient to convert many people to Christianity, including several atheists and agnostics;
- ༄ Biblical testimonies verify the trustworthiness of the Bible, because it reveals the presence of God in the individuals' lives.

Points For Consideration:

- ༄ Do you believe that human beings, apart from God working in their lives can be transformed as the first Century apostles did, and sustain such transformation lifelong?
- ༄ Do you know people, whose lives have been transformed by God?

CHAPTER 6

EVIDENCE # 5: HONESTY OF SCRIPTURE

The honesty of the true Christian Bible is one of those evidences that many people often ignore; yet, the honesty of the Bible points directly to its trustworthiness. The Bible is extremely transparent, almost "to a fault," about the weaknesses and major flaws of the great Saints God used to accomplish His will, especially during the Old Testament era. The Bible reveals the frailty of human beings, including those whom God worked His miracles through. The Bible does not present these individuals as super spiritual, or as possessing special qualities — rather, God chooses people to work through, due in part because of their obedience and willingness to be used by Him.

The significance of the transparency of the Bible is that, the God of the Bible cannot lie; there is no deceit in Him (Numbers 23:19). As such, He tells His story with 100% transparency, revealing to us how in spite of the "fallen human nature", He was with His chosen servants. Because the Bible is inspired by God, this transparency is no accident; it is divinely designed to be transparent. Conversely, other so called Scriptures from all world religions today, which all originate from men, and not from God, are packed with dishonesty and exaggeration about their heroes. Using some examples, let us now examine how transparent the Bible is.

What is the Supporting Evidence For the Honesty of Scripture?

The greatest Saints of the Old Testament had major issues, and the Bible revealed their true natures as "fallen human beings".

Some Old Testament Examples:

As an example, Abraham, the father of all nations, including Jews and Gentiles (non-Jews) alike, a man mightily used by God, was a liar, who lied about his wife at least twice (Genesis 12:11-13, 20:2), for purposes of self preservation. Yet, it was through the man Abraham, that God established His initial covenant (i.e., mutual agreement or contract) with the Jews (see Genesis chapter 15). In spite of his great accomplishment, the Bible revealed how Abraham was a man with many weaknesses, especially evident in His impatience with God, and subsequent corroboration with his wife to have an illegitimate child (see Genesis chapter 16). The Bible did not exaggerate about Abraham's great worth because he was used by God.

As another illustration, Noah , a righteous man in the sight of God during his generation, chosen by God, blessed and given specific instructions to be fruitful and multiply after the massive flood (see Genesis chapters 6 through 9), got drunk after his major divine accomplishment (Genesis 9:20-23). Here again, the Bible did not give us a false impression about the great Saint, Noah; it just revealed to us his weaknesses, yet God worked through him.

Another classic example is seen in the life of Moses. Moses, one of the greatest heroes of the Christian faith, the one who led the children of Israel out of the Egyptian bondage and slavery, the one who received the 10 commandments from the

Evidence #5: Honesty of Scripture

"hand of God" Himself, in addition to the hundreds of other Laws the Jewish Nation had to abide by, the one whom God worked through to manifest His plagues against Pharaoh and the land of Egypt, was a murderer previously to being called by God (see the books of Exodus through Deuteronomy). It is my opinion that, in all of the Old Testament, this man Moses, had the closest encounter with God; yet, he himself did not make it into the promised land because of disobedience (Numbers 20:10-13).

Many times, people read the Bible without taking the time to meditate on what the Lord is teaching us. Just think about this for a moment. If you were to go back and study the books of Genesis through Deuteronomy, you will agree that Moses had an intimate relationship with God. Moses heard the audible voice of God, spent days in His immediate presence, and conversed with God like most of us would converse with our friends. Thus, God thought very highly of Moses as His servant, right? I am certain most of you would say yes. But, in spite of this intimate relationship, God, in His Word, revealed Moses' frailty as a human being. He did not hide it, nor did He present Moses as someone "special," without mistakes. No, He did not, because God cannot lie, regardless of how highly He views His servant. You can trust the Bible as God's Word to you.

Then, there was King David, who was called *"...a man after his [God's] own heart..."* (1 Samuel 13:14), who committed the two major horrible sins against God: murder and adultery, that deserved death according to the Old Testament Law. Yet, God sent the prophet Nathan to expose his lies, and we are told the entire disgraceful story in the Bible (see 2 Samuel chapters 11 and 12). God cannot lie, the Bible is trustworthy, trust it!

We also have Elijah, a major prophet during the Old Testament era, who killed hundreds of Baal's (counterfeit god's) prophets, and called down fire from heaven (see 1 Kings 18); yet, he became grossly fearful, experienced depression, ran away instead of turning to God, and exhibited much carnality when he was threatened by Jezebel (see 1 Kings 19). Elijah was one of the prophets who raised someone from the dead in the Old Testament, something that was not very common during that era. God used Elijah mighty, yet in His Word, God also revealed how Elijah, like most of us, was a fearful and weak man, who had to depend on Him 100%. The Bible is indeed God's story to you.

With regards to the lying, and incidences of murder and other sins associated with some of the Old Testament Saints, or any other individual in the Bible, keep in mind that God never approved of these actions. God will never condone any kind of lies, disobedience, or sin, because He is perfectly holy, and sin cannot abide in His presence. However, the Bible recorded these incidences so that we can learn to avoid them. Also take note that God was still able to work through His chosen servants once they honestly acknowledged their sins, asked for repentance from God, and completely stopped the sin.

Some New Testament Examples:

In the New Testament, as discussed in the previous chapters, Jesus' disciples were fearful, frail and weak individuals, before they were filled with the Holy Spirit. Throughout the apostle Paul's letters to the churches he founded, especially the letter to the church in Corinth (see 1 and 2 Corinthians), we are told about the carnality , emotional and spiritual immaturity of the Saints in that church in Corinth, even though they were true Christians dearly loved by God. God does not attempt to exaggerate the facts, or present a "good face" to the biblical events in order to impress us: He is honest. Only God can be this honest. But humans, in our frailty, would want to impress others by exaggerating the truth and making it favorable in order to elevate our legendary Saints.

::

Furthermore, the Bible is extremely honest about its description of stories of ungodly proportions such as incest, murder, prostitution, etc, even though God did not approve of them.

::

This honesty of the Bible has led many critics of Christianity to incorrectly slander the God of the Bible. Such slandering of God is purely inspired by Satan, in my opinion, because, as already explained, God does not approve these evil deeds: He is just revealing to us the wicked nature of Mankind when they choose to disobey Him and allow Satan to use them. Personally, I really appreciate that God has revealed these stories to us, so we can learn not to repeat them.

Most importantly, we see Jesus Christ, in His humanity (i.e., as a human being, in His nature as a human being), experiencing thirst, hunger, abandonment, etc. Even though Jesus was/is God in the flesh, the Bible did not portray Him as a human being who did not experience the full range of human emotions. The Bible teaches that Jesus Christ was tempted, like any other human being, and He overcame (see Luke chapter 4). Jesus Christ was physically abused and spat on; He wept, just like any other human being (see the Gospels).

It is sad, because here again, in the humanity of Jesus Christ, many Bible critics, who reject that Jesus was 100% God and 100% human being, have criticized that if Jesus was truly God, He would not have experienced all these human emotions. What these critics fail to understand and refuse to accept is the fact that Jesus was/is God 100% and Man 100%, and the Bible is extremely honest in revealing to us, His human nature, 100%. Again, you can trust the Bible 100% because if there was one person that the Bible would have had to lie about, it would have been about the person Jesus Christ, in regards to His human nature. Yet, the Bible tells us as it happened: Jesus did, indeed, experience all of the emotions that we, "fallen human beings" experience daily, but Jesus overcame them all, thus setting a precedence that with the filling of the Holy Spirit, we, as Christians can overcome likewise — Yes, you can trust the Bible as God's inspired Word.

This honesty of the Bible reveals one of God's unique characters, which is consistent throughout the Bible: He cannot lie. No other religious book has this type of honesty in their writings. The books of Mormons and Jehovah's Witnesses' Bible called the New World Translation (NWT) are replete with dishonesty and misrepresentations of the facts; so is the Koran, and the other writings of Hinduism, Chinese Religions, etc. The other religions of the world have taken writings from the Bible and distorted them in order to conform to their theologies.

Summary Points:

- The honesty of the Bible reveals one of God's unique characters: He cannot lie;
- The Bible reveals its great heroes as they are: "fallen human beings" with major flaws.

Points For Consideration:

- What are your thoughts about God's honesty/transparency in His Word? Does it surprise you? If yes, why? If no, why not?
- What do you think about the fact that God still uses weak and frail individuals to accomplish His will?

CHAPTER 7

EVIDENCE #6: NUMBER OF BIBLICAL MANUSCRIPTS

A manuscript is simply a hand written document. But in regards to the Bible, a manuscript is referred to as a "Biblical Document." The number of available biblical manuscripts is another often ignored powerful evidence, that supports the accuracy, reliability and trustworthiness of the Bible. This is relevant because any book hand written by man, has the potential for error, and the Bible is no exception. Thus, studying the thousands of manuscripts of the Bible is absolutely essential, to ascertain its accuracy. Thus, anyone curious about the trustworthiness of the Bible can simply invest some time to do a scrupulous study of the various manuscripts, in order to ascertain the presence of any errors or inconsistencies. But as you will soon learn in the upcoming section, the biblical manuscripts are 100% consistent in their content, and as such reliable, because the teachings encased in the Bible are 100% inspired by God, and can be trusted.

Unfortunately, many critics of the Bible, such as the Muslims and the Mormons espouse that the Bible has been translated and copied so many times over the Centuries, and as such, it cannot be trusted. Well, the interesting thing about the availability of thousands of biblical manuscripts is that, we have, at our disposal, an excellent way to investigate the different manuscripts from the different Centuries, for internal validity and accuracy, with regards to their contents.

However, it appears that the same critics who are quick to criticize the thousands of biblical manuscripts fail to realize that, having the various manuscripts, is in fact, a "blessing in disguise" for the Christian. You know why? Because the same reason they are using to criticize the trustworthiness of the Bible (i.e., the number of available manuscripts), is one of the strongest arguments for the trustworthiness of the Bible as God's Word. Because, as you will soon learn from the upcoming section, in spite of the fact that the biblical manuscripts have been translated and copied many times over the Centuries, God has supernaturally preserved His Word, as all of the manuscripts have supernatural accuracy and unity in content. Thus, time and time again, God has proved His critics to be liars, as the thousands of biblical manuscripts have proven, over hundreds of years, to be 100% accurate and consistent in content. Let us now examine the evidence.

WHAT IS THE SUPPORTING EVIDENCE FOR THE NUMBER OF BIBLICAL MANUSCRIPTS?

There is no other ancient book in the world today, or any ancient book that has ever existed in the history of the world that has as many copies of manuscripts as the Bible.

New Testament Manuscripts:

For example, over 5,000 (five thousand) original Greek New Testament manuscripts such as the Vatican; Sinaitic Codices; Lectionaries; Alexandrian Manuscripts, etc, have been copied over a period of about 100 years, leading to over 25,000 (twenty-five thousand) New Testament manuscripts. This is an amazingly powerful evidence because conversely, other popular writings in the history of the world do not have as many manuscripts as the Bible, for their content to be verified for accuracy and internal consistency.

Evidence #6: Number of Biblical Manuscripts

To illustrate further, other popular ancient books such as Julius Caesar's Gallic Wars, written around first Century B.C.; Plato's writings, written around 3rd to 4th Century B.C.; and Aristotle's poetry, written around 3rd Century B.C., each has less than 50 manuscripts available for scrupulous investigation. As I mentioned earlier, the advantage of having multiple copies of a manuscript is that the copies can be compared against each other for accuracy and reliability, just like it has been done with God's Word: the Bible.

Due to the scrupulous work from Bible scholars in the discipline of Textual Criticism (i.e., the process of examining the biblical manuscripts for any inconsistencies), Biblical manuscripts have undergone millions of hours of textual analysis: cross checking, double checking, and cross examination for errors, accuracy and consistency among the various manuscripts and their reliability to the originals.

Take note that, Textual Criticism does not imply that the biblical text is being criticized; rather, it involves a scrupulous evaluation of Scripture, for purposes of investigating the presence of any potential variances. With such rigorous textual analysis by hundreds of biblical scholars over the Centuries, biblical manuscripts have passed the test with "flying colors," thus attesting to the authenticity of the Bible as God's Word. Yes, you can totally trust the Bible as God's inspired Word to you!

In addition, the New Testament fully endorsed the Old Testament as God's Word, with over 300 citations or quotations from the Old Testament included in the New Testament. The

New Testament writers confirmed the authenticity of the Bible by citing various Old Testament Scriptures. Our Lord Jesus Himself cited the Old Testament Scriptures extensively, and referred people to search the Scripture about Him as the Messiah.

Old Testament Manuscripts:

With regards to the Old Testament manuscripts, Bible scholars have unanimously shown that, the Masoretic Text, which is the name of the hundreds of Old Testament Hebrew Manuscripts copied by Scribes, called Masoretes, and officially dated about A.D. 500, and our contemporary English Bible versions are identical. Besides the Masoretic Text, there are over 10,000 (ten thousand) Old Testament manuscripts, such as, but not limited to, the Samaritan Pentateuch; the Septuagint (i.e., the Greek translation of the Old Testament), done between 250 to 150 B.C.; etc.

Then in 1947, the Dead Sea Scrolls, dated around 200 B.C. to A. D. 100 were discovered, which had almost all of the books of the Old Testament, except the book of Esther. The significance of this discovery is that, the content in the manuscripts found in the Dead Sea Scrolls are identical to our English Bible versions, thus validating the accuracy of God's Word over thousands of years, since it was inspired by God and penned by His chosen servants.

The tedious task of the biblical scholars in the discipline of Textual Criticism have revealed that, after countless hours studying all of the thousands of biblical manuscripts (with the exception of minor differences in spellings and syntax, that is to say, grammar, sentence structure that does not take away from the text), there is a divinely unified accuracy and consistency in all of the manuscripts. Essentially, the primary message of the Bible: God's redemption of Mankind from the fall, the promised Messiah, and the full revelation of God Himself in the person of Jesus Christ, in addition to the hundreds of Christ-centered doctrines taught in the Bible, remains intact. All of these validates the authenticity and accuracy of the Bible as God's Word. Overall, no other religious book in the world has the accuracy, consistency and authenticity after rigorous textual analysis as the Bible, because it is only the Bible that is God inspired. Thus, you can absolutely trust the Bible as God's inspired writings to you!

And here is another interesting twist to this story about biblical manuscripts. Did you know that early Church Fathers, such as Justin Martyr, Eusebius, etc, wrote extensively about the Christian Faith and quoted heavily from the Old and New Testaments? By early Church Father, I am referring to the great men of the Christian Faith, such as, but not limited to Justin Martyr, Eusebius, Polycarp, etc, during the first three Centuries, who wrote and taught extensively about Christianity after the initial disciples of Jesus Christ had all died. The writings of these Church Fathers are still available to us today, and their citations of Scripture are identical to our contemporary Bibles, thus validating the accuracy of God's Word.

As an example of the extent of these Church Fathers' writings, most Bible scholars believe that we can reconstruct today, the entire New Testament, by just studying the writings and quotations from the Church Fathers — this is powerful evidence for the Bible's trustworthiness —you can trust the Bible as God's inspired Word!

Most importantly, the consistency found in the thousands of manuscripts points directly to the presence of God in the process of translating and copying of the Bible in different languages across the different Centuries. This, in and of itself, highlights the permanency of God's Word. It also reveals how God has supernaturally preserved His Word, so that every generation can know of Him (Matthew 24:35)

This is an amazingly good news, and a proof of God's love to us, His creation.

Summary Points:

- No other ancient book in the world exists today compared to the Bible, with as many manuscripts, yet these manuscripts are all consistent;
- Throughout the process of translating and copying of biblical manuscripts, God supernaturally protected and preserved His Word, so that individuals in every generation can know of Him;
- In spite of the thousands of times biblical manuscripts have been translated and copied over the Centuries, the key message of God in the Bible is intact;
- The thousands of Old and New Testament manuscripts have been rigorously analyzed, and have passed the test with "flying colors," with regards to the consistency of the stories they are telling: God's story.

Points For Consideration:

- What do you think about the fact that all of the Bible manuscripts are saying the same thing?

CAN I TRUST THE BIBLE AS GOD'S WORD?

CHAPTER 8

Evidence #7: Consistency of Scripture

As I already explained, archeological evidence lends external validity to the trustworthiness of the Bible. With regards to its internal evidence and consistency, which I have emphasized throughout this book, I am referring to the cohesive nature by which all of the pieces of the Bible fit together, from the book of Genesis to the book of Revelation: the Bible is perfectly consistent in its teachings and themes.

This consistency of the Bible in and of itself is supernatural.

Human beings are the ones who interpret the Bible incorrectly, thus leading to much confusion in interpretation, but the teachings and themes of the Bible are absolutely 100% supernaturally consistent.

It is my belief that any honest student of the Bible would agree with this statement. There are hundreds of consistent themes in the Bible, but due to space limitation in this book, I am only able to discuss a few. Below are some examples:

What is the Supporting Evidence For the Consistency of Scripture?

1. The Bible is written by over 40 different authors across different parts of the world, during different Centuries, yet these authors are extremely consistent in their message about God the Father, God the Son, and God the Holy Spirit, and God's plan for redemption. This is an amazing fact, just think about this for a moment!

The chosen individuals God used to write down His Word lived in different parts of the world, with different occupations, such as Fishermen (e.g., most of Jesus' apostles); a Shepherd (e.g., King David); a Scholar (e.g., the apostle Paul); a tax collector (e.g., Matthew); and others were Prophets (e.g., Jeremiah; Samuel); etc. They also wrote the books of the Bible across different parts of the world. As an example, Moses wrote the book of Genesis in the wilderness, in the Sinai Peninsula; the apostle Paul wrote several books, such as the book of Romans, while in prison in Rome; the apostle John wrote the book of Revelation while on exile in the Island of Patmos for preaching Christ; Ezekiel wrote his book while under Babylonian captivity; etc. Yet, all of these writers were 100% consistent in their writings, because they were all inspired and guided by the Holy Spirit —This is amazingly supernatural! Only God can do this, period!

Conversely, no other religious book in the history of the world was written by several authors with such divine consistency, except the Bible. For example, other world religious books, such as the Koran, is written by just one person, Muhammad, and it contains his vision, which is distorted and not even corroborated. The Book of Mormon is written by one person, Joseph Smith, with no verifiable eye witnesses; again, it is just his vision, which is subjective, biased and falsified. It is the same thing with the Jehovah's Witnesses Bible, called New World Translation, which is Charles Russell's primary vision, and is packed with falsified data and interpretations.

2. The Bible is written by authors who spoke three different languages: Hebrew, Aramaic and Greek, yet they are consistent in their message, the progressive revelation of the Triune God. This is another amazing presence of God in guiding and directing the writings of His Word. How do you explain the fact that, the different authors who wrote the Bible spoke different languages, lived in different Centuries across different parts of the world, yet they all wrote down the same thing? The Bible is undeniably the work of God.

3. The revelation of God in the Old Testament (Old Covenant), although progressive, is the same revelation we find in the New Testament, except it is a full revelation in the New Covenant, in the person of Jesus Christ. Here again, how do you explain the fact that, the Old Testament prophets who lived hundreds of years before some of the New Testament Saints were even born, all wrote about the same qualities and/or attributes of the God of the Bible? You know why? Because God revealed it to them, The only true living God is the God of the Bible. The Bible can be trusted! No other religious book in the world has this kind of consistency.

4. The nature and character of God is consistent across the Testaments, again this revelation was partial in the Old Testament, and now it is complete in the person of Jesus Christ in the New Testament.

5. The love of God, His grace, righteousness, faithfulness, etc, are all qualities of God that the inspired writers of the Bible revealed across the Testaments.

6. The Bible is also very consistent about addressing the greatest issues experienced by Mankind, and is 100% consistent across the Testaments in its solutions. Some of these issues include, but are not limited to: (1) whether or not God exists, and how to have a relationship with Him; (2) who created the universe; (3) how sin and death came about; (4) why Jesus came into the world; (5) how to live a holy life pleasing to God; (6) the issue of evil in the world; (7) how to accomplish your divine purpose in this life; (8) what happens when you die; (9) how this present world will end; (10) the permanent destruction of Satan and his evil deeds; etc.

I could easily write an entire book about this issue of biblical consistency, but suffice it to say that, the above discussion speaks for itself, in validating the trustworthiness of the Bible. It would have been humanly impossible for the pieces of the Bible to perfectly fit together, given the different geographical locations and Centuries in which the different writers lived, if the Bible was not inspired by God!

The Bible not only addresses every possible human condition we encounter in this life, but God, in His love, foresaw our predicament as "fallen human beings", and gave His inspired Word to us as encased in the Bible, as a guide to use. No wonder, the Bible is the number one selling book of all time.

Evidence #7: Consistency of Scripture

The message in the Bible is timeless, it transcends every culture, race, ethnicity, gender, government, civilization, and generation. No other religious book can make such a claim of internal consistency as the Bible. Trust the Bible as God's Word to you!

Summary Points:

- ɞ The Bible's internal consistency in and of itself is supernatural: it can only be from God;
- ɞ No other so called religious book in the history of the world has the supernatural internal consistency that the Bible has, because only the Bible is inspired by God;
- ɞ The revelation of God in the Bible is 100% consistent across the Old and New Testaments.

Points For Consideration:

- ɞ What do you think about the fact that the other religious books do not have the internal consistency, such as we find in the Bible, yet they are called "Holy"?
- ɞ What do you think about the supernatural consistency of the Holy Scripture? Does it surprise you?

CHAPTER 9

EVIDENCE #8:
EXTRA BIBLICAL WRITINGS

Extra biblical writings may also be grouped in the same category as archeological evidence, but I discuss them separately here. By extra biblical writings, I am referring to the writings of various historians, Christians and non-Christians alike throughout various Centuries, whose writings have corroborated with the names and events mentioned in the Bible. These extra biblical writings are historical writings pertaining to events in the world, and are not considered Scriptural. Nonetheless, these writings provide a means by which events, names and places mentioned in the Bible can be verified, to ascertain if they "line- up" with history, as the Bible espouses.

Since the Bible is written in the context of history, this should not be very surprising, right? Although, some of you may not be aware that there are multiple other writings besides the Bible that talks about the same individuals and events as described in the Bible. Thus, being that the Bible is written in the context of world history, it lends itself to scrupulous examination, whether or not some of the stories described in the Bible actually took place.

There are hundreds of historical writings that have corroborated biblical accounts of events, but due to space limitations, I can only discuss a few of them here. Extra biblical writings from sources such as the Romans; Jews (i.e., the Jewish Talmud); Babylonians, Assyrians; etc, do verify the accuracy of biblical events, names and places. Let us briefly examine some of these writings.

What is the Supporting Evidence For Extra Biblical Writings?

As an example, the Babylonian chronicles, which are records of ancient Babylonian history, records information that is consistent with the Bible. Its recording includes the rise to power of King Nebuchadnezzar; the story about Nebuchadnezzar's siege of Jerusalem around 586 B.C.; and the capturing of the Jews; all these writings are consistent with biblical rendering of the same events as recorded in the Old Testament texts.

Also, noted famous first Century historian, Flavius Josephus, wrote extensively about the Jewish people and their culture, and his writings can be found in what is called the *"Antiquities of the Jews."* In his writings, Josephus discussed events surrounding the ministry of our Lord Jesus, including His crucifixion and death, in addition to discussing several other names of individuals discussed in the Bible, such as Felix; Herod the Great; Festus; Caiaphas; Pontius Pilate; John the Baptist; James "the brother of our Lord Jesus" (see the Book of Acts; the Gospels); etc.

As an illustration, in his writings, Josephus wrote about the execution of John the Baptist, which the Bible teaches as an event that actually happened. Josephus noted:

"...Now some of the Jews thought that the destruction of Herod's army came from God, and that very justly, as a punishment of what he did against John, that was called

the Baptist: for Herod slew him, who was a good man, and commanded the Jews to exercise virtue, both as to righteousness towards one another, and piety towards God..." (Antiquities of the Jews, 18: 116).

Furthermore, Josephus also wrote about the death of James, the brother of the Lord Jesus. As you read his account below, take note that the Bible teaches us this historical fact as well (see Acts Chapter 12). Josephus corroborated the biblical account, he wrote:

"...so he assembled the Sanhedrim of judges, and brought before them the brother of Jesus, who was called Christ, whose name was James, and some others, [or, some of his companions]; and when he had formed an accusation against them as breakers of the law, he delivered them to be stoned..."(Antiquities of the Jews, 20: 9).

And in his writing about our Lord Jesus Christ, Josephus stated:

..."Now there was about this time Jesus, a wise man, if it be lawful to call him a man; for he was a doer of wonderful works, a teacher of such men as receive the truth with pleasure. He drew over to him both many of the Jews and many of the Gentiles. He was [the] Christ. And when Pilate, at the suggestion of the principal men amongst us, had condemned him to the cross, those that loved him at the first did not forsake him; for he appeared to them alive again the third day; as the divine prophets had foretold these and ten thousand other wonderful things concerning him. And the tribe of Christians, so named from him, are not extinct at this day...." (Antiquities of the Jews, 18: 63).

Please take note that Josephus, in his writings above, is describing details and names pertaining to our Lord's death, that are 100% consistent with biblical account. Additionally, it is noteworthy to know that, this renown first Century Jewish historian, Josephus, was not even a follower of Christ —he was just a historian, writing about world events during his era. But as you can see for yourself from his writings above, his recording of events are very much consistent with Scripture.

Other significant events discussed in the Bible that have been corroborated by historians include but are not limited to the:

- ✓ Genesis flood;

- ✓ Darkness and earthquake that occurred after the death of our Lord on the cross;

- ✓ Sudden death of Herod Agrippa' after being honored as a god;

- ✓ Names of historical figures mentioned in the Bible, such as King David; Pontius Pilate; etc.

Some of you may be struggling with accepting the above extra biblical sources. But to this end, I have a few questions for you: *Do you believe that George Washington, the first president of the United States of America actually existed? And do you believe that Saddam Hussein lived on this earth?* If your response is yes, to the two questions asked, then, don't you think that historians who lived along side these notable world figures discussed in the Bible would have written about them as well? Of course yes! Most of you would agree with me.

Likewise, events, as written in the Bible, which took place in world history, were also recorded by historians during that time and beyond, and their writings, which corroborated

Evidence #8: Extra Biblical Writings

biblical events, have added validity to the trustworthiness of the Bible, and have proven, again, that skeptics are wrong.

::

Thus, along with archeological evidences validating events, places and names of biblical accounts, the extra biblical writings lend added credibility to the trustworthiness of the Bible. The Bible can be trusted.

::

SUMMARY POINTS:

- ༨ The writings of countless Christians and non Christian historians alike over the last hundreds of years have corroborated countless events, names and individuals mentioned in the Bible;
- ༨ Only the true Christian Bible has such validated and corroborated historical evidence, as discussed above, aligning and consistent with world history. No other religious book in the history of the world has such authenticated evidence to support its claims: except the Bible.

POINTS FOR CONSIDERATION:

- ༨ What are your thoughts about the consistent nature of the extra biblical accounts, compared with those of the Bible? What surprises you the most?

CHAPTER 10

EVIDENCE #9: SCIENTIFIC ACCURACY

The Bible is not a scientific book. God does not need to prove Himself, because faith is what pleases Him; He wants you to accept Him by faith (Hebrews 11: 6). So do not waste your time to compare the Bible with your scientific data and attempt to prove or disprove the Bible. In the Bible, individuals used unscientific "layman's language" to describe our current earth, rather than scientific or astrological terminologies, but this does not nullify the accuracy of the description. As an example, the apostle John used simple to understand "layman's language" to describe the four cardinal directions: North, South, East and West of the earth; in Revelation 7:1, he described it as "the four corners of the earth."

While the Bible has the scientific evidence to support God's account of creation, comparing the Bible with a scientific book is a futile attempt.

What God has done in the Bible is to simply tell us about the world in which we live in, in regards to the stars; the shape of the earth; the valleys; the seas; etc, long before scientists made these discoveries. And with subsequent scientific discoveries since the creation of the universe, the Bible has been accurate in its description. So in a nutshell, science cannot, and does not prove God, but science agrees with the Bible. Below are some of the supporting evidence.

WHAT IS THE SUPPORTING EVIDENCE FOR SCIENTIFIC ACCURACY?

The Bible has numerous evidence to support God's account of creation, below are just a few of them:

- **The shape of the Earth as Circular**

As an example, before scientists were even born, God revealed to us in His Word that the earth was circular. Here is how God puts it: *"Do you not know? Have you not heard? Has it not been told you from the beginning? Have you not understood since the earth was founded? He sits enthroned **above the circle of the earth**, and its people are like grasshoppers. He stretches out the heavens like a canopy, and spreads them out like a tent to live in"* (Isaiah 40: 21-22), (emphasis author's). This information was already revealed in the Bible before scientists discovered it, thus authenticating the Bible as God's inspired book.

- **The Innumerable Stars and Sand**

God further revealed in His Word: He took him (referring to Abram) outside and said, *"Look up at the sky and count the stars—if indeed you can count them."* Then he said to him, *"So shall your offspring be"* (Genesis 15: 5). Also, God told us: " *I will make the descendants of David my servant and the Levites who minister before me as countless as the stars in the sky and as measureless as the sand on the seashore"* (Jeremiah 33:22), (emphasis author's). God knew before the scientists that the skies and sand cannot be counted.

Evidence #9: Scientific Accuracy

- **The Presence of Valleys in the Seas**

    God also said: *"The valleys of the sea were exposed and the foundations of the earth laid bare at the rebuke of the Lord, at the blast of breath from his nostrils"* (2 Samuel 22:16), (emphasis author's). The Bible tells us the origins of the Valleys and Seas, in addition to their location before scientists found out.

- **The Earth Suspends Over Nothing**

    For Centuries, other religions and even some philosophers believed that the earth was suspended on "something," but around the 16th Century, scientific discoveries revealed that the earth is suspended on nothing, just as revealed in the Bible: *"He spreads out the northern skies over empty space; he suspends the earth over nothing"* (Job 26:7), (emphasis author's).

- **The Exact Direction of the Sun, Stars, and Seas**

    God ordered the movement of His creation before scientific discoveries, He stated:

"... he who appoints the sun to shine by day, who decrees the moon and stars to shine by night, who stirs up the sea so that its waves roar— the Lord Almighty is his name..." (Jeremiah 31:35), (emphasis author's).

Also, scientists now agree, after years of disagreement, that God is right in telling us in His Word that the sun is in a circuit through space. The Bible teaches in Psalm 19:

"It rises at one end of the heavens and makes its circuit to the other; nothing is deprived of its warmth "(v. 6), (emphasis author's).

- **The Origin and Nature of Living Organisms**

    Before biologists figured out the origins of human organism and the pattern, God had already revealed it to us in His Word: *"Then God said, "Let the land produce vegetation: seed-bearing plants and trees on the land that bear fruit with seed in it, according to their various kinds." And it was so. The land produced vegetation: plants bearing seed according to their kinds and trees bearing fruit with seed in it according to their kinds. And God saw that it was good"* (Genesis 1:11-12), (emphasis author's).

    Scientists now know that there are living creatures in the sea, but God told us first: *"So God created the great creatures of the sea and every living thing with which the water teems and that moves about in it, according to their kinds, and every winged bird according to its kind. And God saw that it was good"*(Genesis 1:21), (emphasis author's).

    God also told us about origins of animals: *"God made the wild animals according to their kinds, the livestock according to their kinds, and all the creatures that move along the ground according to their kinds. And God saw that it was good"* (Genesis 1:25), (emphasis author's). In fact, God told this information to the scientists, then they went searching for it.

- **The Movement of Water and the Vastness of the Sea**

    God tells us exactly how water circulates: *" All streams flow into the sea, yet the sea is never full. To the place the streams come from, there they return again"* (Ecclesiastes 1:7), (emphasis author's).

There are other scientific evidence, such as those pertaining to human physiology, physical health and medicine that are consistent with the Bible, which due to space limitation, I cannot expound on. But here are just a few examples, the Bible teaches that human life is in the blood (Leviticus 17: 11), and science and medicine both agree. The Bible teaches that: " *A cheerful heart is good medicine, but a crushed spirit dries up the bones*" (Proverbs 17:22), (emphasis author's), and medical research has shown a strong correlation between good health and laughter, thus validating the Bible.

The Bible further teaches that: " *Gracious words are a honeycomb, sweet to the soul and healing to the bones*" (Proverbs 16:24), and medical research has validated this truth by showing a very strong correlation between meditating on God's gracious Words and improved health. Suffice it to say that, while some atheist scientists have attempted to disprove the Bible, their research has in fact added credibility to the facts and accuracy of the Bible. Amazing how God works! You can indeed trust the Bible as God's Word to you!

Summary Points:

- ❧ Science cannot prove or disprove the Bible, but scientific discoveries over the Centuries have been consistent with biblical writings and facts about the earth, human biology, origins of animals and other creatures;
- ❧ All of the discovered scientific evidence adds credibility to the trustworthiness of the Bible: You can trust the Bible.

Points For Consideration:

- ❧ What are your thoughts about the scientific accuracy about the earth, as described by the Bible?
- ❧ What are your thoughts about the fact that God's Word has proven that the scientists who disagree with Him have been wrong, all along?

CHAPTER 11

EVIDENCE # 10: THE RESURRECTION OF JESUS CHRIST

A plethora of books have been written about the resurrection of our Lord Jesus Christ, thus in this section, I will only focus on the significance of the resurrection in regards to the authenticity of the Bible. Before I proceed with this brief discussion about the resurrection of the Lord Jesus, some basic background information is necessary, for clarification. Those of you interested in an in-depth study about our Lord Jesus Christ should check out the resource list at the end of this book, in order to obtain my book titled: **"Answers to the Toughest 25 Questions About the Real Jesus,"** for details. I begin with some definitions of the different names and titles of our Lord Jesus, because in the Jewish culture, especially during biblical times, birth names had great significance.

In the Bible, our Lord is addressed as Jesus Christ, and at times as the *Messiah*, although our Lord often referred to Himself as *Son of Man* (see the Gospels), emphasizing His humanity. *Jesus*, the Hebrew name for Joshua, means *"Savior."* *Christ*, in Greek means Messiah, meaning *"the anointed one."* Our Lord was also referred to as: *Immanuel,* at the time of His birth (Matthew 1:23), meaning *" God with us."* Another title of our Lord Jesus was *Son of God* (see the Gospels), referring to His Deity, given His unique relationship with the Father, God.

So as described above, all of the names and titles point us to no ordinary human being; but rather, to God Himself. Jesus, who was God Himself in the form of a human being (i.e., God Incarnate, meaning God supernaturally became a human being in the person of Jesus Christ; see the Gospels), was a real person in history, who lived in time and space in this world over 2,000 years ago exactly as documented in the Gospels.

Unfortunately, some individuals, such as devout atheists, Richard Dawkins, have expressed doubts if Jesus Christ was a real person or just a myth. As discussed already, extra biblical writings from renown historians such as Flavius Josephus and other Jewish rabbis who were not even followers of Jesus Christ wrote extensively about Him — Yes indeed, our Lord and Savior Jesus Christ existed as a historical individual in this world, and had a ministry on this earth. He was crucified on the cross, and died, but on the third day, God the Father raised Him from the dead. Let us now briefly examine the evidence and His supernatural testimony.

WHAT IS THE SUPPORTING EVIDENCE FOR THE RESURRECTION OF JESUS CHRIST?

Among all the evidences available to us today for the authenticity and trustworthiness of the Bible as God's Word, it is my opinion that the resurrection of our Lord and Savior Jesus Christ from the dead is by far the most significant. Jesus Christ is the only person in this life who has ever prophesied about His death, burial, and resurrection, and it happened exactly as He said it would (Matthew 12:40; Mark 8:31). Refer to preceding chapters of this book for details about prophecies pertaining to Him. In First Corinthians chapter 15, under the inspiration of the Holy Spirit, the apostle Paul explains to the believers in Corinth, including us, today:

Evidence #10: The Resurrection of Jesus Christ

If there is no resurrection of the dead, then not even Christ has been raised. And if Christ has not been raised, our preaching is useless and so is your faith. More than that, we are then found to be false witnesses about God, for we have testified about God that he raised Christ from the dead. But he did not raise him if in fact the dead are not raised. For if the dead are not raised, then Christ has not been raised either. **And if Christ has not been raised, your faith is futile; you are still in your sins.** *Then those also who have fallen asleep in Christ are lost. If only for this life we have hope in Christ, we are of all people most to be pitied.* **But Christ has indeed been raised from the dead**, *the first fruits of those who have fallen asleep. For since death came through a man, the resurrection of the dead comes also through a man. For as in Adam all die, so in Christ all will be made alive* (vv. 13-22), (emphasis author's).

While the concept of resurrection may be too difficult for some people to accept, the resurrection of Jesus was a real event that happened in history. After His resurrection, the Lord Jesus appeared to over 500 people who were credible eye witnesses and attested to have seen the "Risen Christ." And at the time the apostle Paul wrote to the Corinthians as recorded in the Bible, some of those eye witnesses were still alive to corroborate his story. The "Risen Christ" also appeared to His disciples and to the apostle Paul himself (see 1 Corinthians 15).

No other religious leader in the history of the world has ever been dead, buried, and raised from the dead , except Jesus Christ. Conversely, the burial sites of Muhammad, of the Islamic faith; Krishna, of the Hinduism religion; Confucius, of the Chinese religion, and all other religious leaders in the world today, and those from the past, still have their remains in their burial sites: they are still dead. But the followers of Jesus Christ, true Christians, serve a God who is alive. **The tomb of Jesus Christ is empty because He is not dead; He is risen**

, **just like the Bible recorded: this authenticates the Bible 100% as the Word of God.**

Because Jesus was raised from the dead, we , His followers, have hope that we too, will be raised from the dead when we die, and we will be reunited with our loved ones who died as Christians. This is the best hope there is: No other religion in the world offers their followers such authenticated hope; this is only found in the Bible. The resurrection of Jesus Christ was such a significant event in world history that it prompted the change of the calendar system from BC (before Christ), to AD (Anno Domini, meaning the year of our Lord).

The resurrection, along with Jesus' miracles proved and validated the testimony of Jesus Christ as the Messiah: the only way to God, and provides supernatural credibility and trustworthiness for the Bible. Like I said at the opening of this section, if the resurrection was the only evidence there is about the trustworthiness of the Bible, it would be sufficient for me to trust it. And countless others, across the various Centuries have become Christians, just based on the proven, verifiable and authenticated evidence of the resurrection of Jesus Christ.

Unfortunately, in an attempt to deny true Christianity and its claims to be the only true faith, many critics and other religious groups, influenced by Satan, in my opinion, have come up with all sorts of ridiculous lies to discredit the resurrection.

::

One thing is clear: these critics of the resurrection have the burden of proof, not Christians ; meaning, they have to show us the physical body of Jesus Christ, then we can talk, otherwise, end of discussion, period! Because Jesus is risen, and is alive!

::

Evidence #10: The Resurrection of Jesus Christ

I can easily tell all other religions in the world where the remains of their leaders can be found. But not with Jesus, He is real; He is the only way to God! And He desires a relationship with you today! Because He died for you.

The resurrection of the Lord Jesus is one of the central Truths about the Christian faith, and it is the key Truth that sets true Christianity apart from other man-made world religions.

Summary Points:

- Because of Jesus Christ, every true Christian will also be resurrected and be reunited with their loved ones who died as Christians;
- The resurrection of Jesus Christ remains the number one reason that has drawn countless individuals throughout the various Centuries to become His ardent followers.

Points For Consideration:

- What do you think about the fact that for Centuries, critics of Christianity have fabricated stories to disqualify the resurrection of Jesus, but to no avail?
- If the resurrection of Jesus was the only evidence available for the trustworthiness of the Bible, would you trust the Bible? If no, Why not?

CHAPTER 12

BE A DOER OF THE WORD

Now that you have, hopefully come into agreement with God that His Word, as encased in the Bible is trustworthy, only one thing is necessary: practicing what the Word of God teaches. Believing in God , His Word, and studying the Bible are all great, but the Bible is clear that only those who practice what the Bible teaches receive God's blessings. Here is how the Lord Jesus puts it in Luke chapter 6:

"Why do you call me, 'Lord, Lord,' and do not do what I say? As for everyone who comes to me and hears my words and puts them into practice, I will show you what they are like. They are like a man building a house, who dug down deep and laid the foundation on rock. When a flood came, the torrent struck that house but could not shake it, because it was well built. **But the one who hears my words and does not put them into practice is like a man who built a house on the ground without a foundation.** *The moment the torrent struck that house, it collapsed and its destruction was complete"* (vv. 46-49), (emphasis author's).

In the above Scripture, the Lord is teaching us that:

- ❖ To be His true followers or disciples, we must practice what He teaches;

- ❖ His teachings, as expressed throughout the Holy Scripture, are the only Truths than can enable us to undergo the hardships in this present world, because **there is only one Truth, the Truth in God's Words.**

All other so called truths are man-made inventions, philosophies and ideologies that cannot withstand the evil and hardship that are evident in this present fallen world;

❖ Those who do not practice His Word, referring to all of His teachings in the Bible, will definitely, not be able to sustain the inevitable hardships, trials, and tribulations that this world has to offer; thus, they will eventually fail, in all of their endeavors.

So the Lord Jesus, our God and Savior, has left us with only one choice: to study and practice His teachings, if we want to overcome in this dark world as His disciples.

Then under the inspiration of the Holy Spirit, the apostle James wrote about the necessity of being a practitioner of the Word of God. He wrote:

"Do not merely listen to the word, and so deceive yourselves. Do what it says. Anyone who listens to the word but does not do what it says is like someone who looks at his face in a mirror and, after looking at himself, goes away and immediately forgets what he looks like. But whoever looks intently into the perfect law that gives freedom, and continues in it—not forgetting what they have heard, but doing it—they will be blessed in what they do" (James 1:22-25), (emphasis author's).

As the above Scriptures teach, the Word of God is described as **"the perfect law"**, which brings deliverance from all sorts of physical, emotional and spiritual bondages, and freedom in the lives of those who practice it. If all you do is to just listen and/or read the Word, and fail to practice what it teaches, you will be like a person who does not remember what he or she looks like, yet goes around, deceiving him or herself

—what a horrible description of those who do not practice God's Word. Most importantly, the apostle James reiterated the teaching of our Lord, as he highlighted that, only those who practice what the Word of God teaches receive God's blessings in this life.

So, it is obvious that practicing the Word of God is the primary way that we, God's children can receive anything from Him. I have ministered to countless individuals, who claim to love God, but unfortunately, they just do not practice what the Bible teaches nor obey God's Word; but yet, they are expecting Godly results in their lives. I am sorry to say that it does not work like this:

the only way to experience Godly results, such as peace, joy, deliverance from all sorts of fears, worry, ungodly relationships, financial hardships, etc, is to obey God and practice what He teaches in His Word, period!

You cannot compromise with this. With God, there is no compromising or half-hearted commitment: you are either committed 100% towards the things of God, or you are not, that's it —non-negotiable!

Do You Really Want to Practice God's Word?

Before I proceed, I want to simply ask you a few questions: *Do you really want to know the God of the Bible?* And, do you really want to practice what He teaches in the Bible? These are very relevant questions, because many people who claim to want to know God, really do not want to invest the time in knowing Him! They only say so because they want others to believe that they are godly people.

As an example, there is this lady that I have been witnessing to for over 1 year now. She actually purchased some of my books and other materials, claiming she wants to know the Lord more. But just a few weeks ago, I ran into her, and upon talking with her in order to ascertain whether or not she is finally "walking" with the Lord, her response amazed me. *She looked at me and said "where is God, and how do I know this God"?* I was not impressed with her response, and I immediately confronted her hypocrisy.

I looked at her, straight into her eyes and boldly told her this: *" you know in your heart you do not want to know God. You know you are lying, because I have spent over a year teaching and telling you about God, but you are not interested; just be honest, and stop playing this game with your life."* After I said this, she looked down on the floor in embarrassment, and acknowledged that she lied. She went on to explain that she has not even read the books and other materials she got from our ministry about knowing God. She then thanked me for all the time I had ministered to her about God, and she agreed that I have done my part, but she is not ready.

I could give you many other examples to this effect, but you get the point. I only brought up this example to highlight how, "talk is cheap", and God is not impressed with just mere talk. Besides, He knows your heart anyway, so you might as well be honest (Acts 15:8; Jeremiah 17:9-10). And most importantly, there is a cardinal biblical truth that if you truly desire to know God, He will reveal more of Himself to you (Jeremiah 29:12-14).

So, *do you really want* to know *God*? If yes, then, the best way to know Him is through His written Word, because the Word of God is God, and God is His Word, you cannot separate them! Even though God has already revealed Himself to us through nature, and through our consciences (see Romans chapter 1; 14), His written Word is the best and primary way to know the God of the Bible. Unfortunately, there are many individuals who want a vision, or a dream, or even an audible voice before obeying God, rather than trusting and relying on His Word.

Firstly, if God chooses to speak to you through a dream, a vision, or an audible voice, it will be 100% consistent with His revealed Word in the Bible, because we do not serve a God of confusion or disorder: the God of the Bible is 100% consistent (1 Corinthians 14:33). Secondly, God will not reveal to you any new information/revelation about your circumstance or any other situation, because His Word has the complete (100%) counsel/solution for everything we, as Christians, need to live in this world (2 Timothy 3:16). Thus, God is not revealing new information to us today; He has already revealed all that we need to know, as encased in the Bible. Thirdly, relying on visions, dreams, or an audible voice can be dangerous, because your enemy, Satan, can manifest himself in a vision, a dream, or even speak to you in an audible voice and deceive you (2 Corinthians 11:12-14). But, if you know the Word of God, Satan will have a very difficult time deceiving you.

Hence, for the individual who really wants to know the God of the Bible, or the true Christian who wants to draw closer to God and practice His decrees, the Bible is the best, and the only reliable source to help you with this endeavor.

But, in order to know God and practice what He is teaching you in the Scriptures, it is necessary that you learn how to study His Word in the first place.

To this effect, below, I have offered some basic recommendations on how to begin a basic study of God's Word. Those interested in details about studying the Word of God can obtain my book titled: **"Are You Moving Forward with Jesus? How to Excel in Your Identity in Christ,"** where I dedicated several chapters discussing how to study and apply God's Word into your life and expect godly results. So check the resource list at the end of this book on how to obtain that book. Here are the basic recommendations:

Some Basic Recommendations On How to Study the Bible

- *Act on Your Sincere Desire to Know God's Word*

This is where it all begins. If you are sincere in your heart about wanting to know God, then act on that desire and get serious. Purchase a study Bible such as the New International Version (NIV); New King James Version (NKJV); New Living Translation (NLT); etc. But remember, do not get the Jehovah's Witnesses falsified Bible called New World Translation (NWT).

Consider getting a couple of different Bible translations. As an example, you could get the NIV as your main study Bible, then the NLT as another study Bible. Additionally, consider getting an easy to read Bible for your devotional study, such as the Living Bible. The biggest advantage of having multiple translations of the Bible is that, it will add clarity to your study, as it will enable you to study how different Bible translations render different verses of the Bible. Remember that, through the discipline of Textual Criticism, and God's preservation of His Word, you can trust our contemporary English Bible translations, as they are all saying the same thing in different ways. Today, there are many other resources such as Bible dictionaries, concordances, Lexicons, various internet programs, etc, that can help you to better understand the Bible; invest in some of these, it will be worth it!

- *Ask the Holy Spirit for Revelation Before You Begin*

I highly recommend that you never begin your study of the Bible without first praying for revelation. Remember, the Holy Spirit inspired the Holy Scriptures, and the same Holy Spirit will supernaturally illuminate His Words to you (i.e., give you revelation knowledge, and/or give you a supernatural understanding of what you are studying). Because without having a basic revelation of what the Scripture is teaching, you will experience difficulty putting it to practice in your life. So, if you truly desire to understand God's Word, then trust the Holy Spirit to speak to your heart as you study — He will, for sure!

- *Have A Note Book With You*

Attempt to always have a notebook with you before you begin your study of God's Word, in order to write down your thoughts. Always approach the Scripture with expectation and confidence, believing that God will teach you something about Himself, and about life in general. As an example, before you begin studying any passage of Scripture or book of the Bible, write down these 4 questions on your notebook: (1) what will God teach me in this passage of Scripture or book about Himself, others, or living as a Christian? (2) based on this passage of Scripture or book, is there something in my life I can change? Or, is there something in my life I need to repent about? (3) what will God teach me in this passage of Scripture or book about treating others? (4) how can I apply the Truths found in the Scriptures in my life, today? I guarantee you, if you approach Scripture with just these basic questions, you will definitely have a lot to write down on your notebook by the time you are through with your study, which will in turn enable you to put it to practice.

Also, keep in mind that for the most part, most of the teachings in the Bible are straight forward and simple; but it is us, human beings, who make it complicated because we fail to acknowledge the simplicity in God's Word. Thus, approach God's Word with an open heart, believing that God will speak to you in a simplistic manner, and He will; do not make it complicated, it is not! And make it a habit to ask the Holy Spirit to teach you how to apply His Truths daily, in your life.

- *Begin With the Gospel of John*

Start here, in order to know more about Jesus Christ as your personal Lord , Savior and friend. Next, study the short, but powerful epistles of 1st, 2nd, and 3rd John, as these will speak to your heart about God's kind of love, and teach you how to detect a counterfeit so called Christianity. Love is the cardinal trait of the true Christian, thus having a revelation of God's unconditional love to you is paramount in your relationship with Him, and on how you can in turn "walk" in love towards others. Hence, the epistles of John will help you with this endeavor.

Thereafter, go to the Old Testament and read the book of Genesis, to learn how it all started. Then, as you are led by the Holy Spirit, read the rest of the Bible, from the book of Genesis to the book of Revelation. If you need help with studying through the entire Bible, our ministry has an in-depth audio Podcast series, that focuses on teaching through the entire

Bible, from the book of Genesis to the book of Revelation. If you are interested in this Podcast, you can subscribe to it and grow in God's Word.

- *Never Study the Bible Out of Context*

This is a major principle in studying the Bible. Studying the Bible out of context is the primary reason why we have pseudo Christian cults today, such as the Jehovah's Witnesses and the Mormons. Also, it is the primary reason why so many godly Christians are not experiencing God's blessings in their lives. This topic is so involved that, in this book, I am unable to expound on this very relevant issue. But suffice it to say that, you should always:

I. Read a few chapters or verses before and after the particular passage of Scripture you are interested in. For example, if you are interested in studying Genesis chapter 4, begin by studying Genesis chapter 3 and chapter 5. Better yet, begin at Genesis chapter 1, then read through to Genesis chapter 3, then focus on Genesis chapter 4; additionally, proceed to Genesis chapter 5. Doing this will give you a contextual perspective about Genesis chapter 4, your chapter of interest;

II. If you are interested in a topical study, such as "walking in biblical faith", Hebrews chapter 11 will be an excellent place to start. Here again, you will study Hebrews chapter 10 and Hebrews chapter 12, in order to get a contextual perspective of how the writer of the book of Hebrews is teaching us about biblical faith;

III. Then, you will approach this topic of faith from the totality of Scripture; meaning, you will want to understand what the other books of the Bible are teaching about biblical faith. To do this therefore, you will study books such as the book of James, focusing on chapters 1 through 3; other New Testament books, such as the Gospel accounts, studying how various individuals exhibited faith in God. Additionally, you will study other Old Testament texts, focusing on the faith of various Saints, such as Abraham, Moses, Joshua, etc.

While the task of studying the Scripture contextually may appear daunting to some of you, keep in mind that once you embark on this endeavor once, it will become easier each time you approach the Scriptures. And most importantly, you will obtain a correct, and a richer perspective and revelation of God's Word, and then putting it to practice will be much easier.

- *Learn to Meditate on God's Word*

By meditation, I am not referring to a casual studying or reading of the Bible. Also, for the Christian, meditation is not the same thing as the Transcendental Meditation that is practiced by various Eastern Religions, such as Buddhism, Hinduism, etc, for purposes of emptying the mind. Rather, to the Christian, meditation involves a deliberate (1) studying of God's Word; (2) pondering on His Truths and wisdom; (3) asking relevant questions to God about the text you are studying; and (4) purposefully thinking about the Truths in the Scriptures over a prolonged period of time, until God's Truths' become your reality. This endeavor can take some time, but it is through the practice of meditation that you will gain much insight about God's Word.

As part of meditating, you can also write down Scriptures on a 4 by 4 card and carry it with you throughout the day, and then focus on those Scriptures, and think about them over, and over, and over again! And as you do this, God will definitely speak to you through those Scriptures. Also, while meditating, envision yourself as already overcoming whatever issues and/or problems you are experiencing, because you are already a winner in Christ, and your enemy, Satan, is attempting to steal from you, do not allow him!

Some of you may be thinking that meditation is too much work. But it is not! All of us meditate, all of the time. Except, some of you meditate on your problems (i.e., you think about your problems over and over), rather than meditate on the solutions: God's Word. So, in the same way that you would normally meditate on your problems, reverse that process, and instead, meditate on the solutions found in the Holy Scriptures. My book titled: **Are You Moving Forward with Jesus? How to Excel in Your Identity in Christ,"** has more teaching about meditation. If you need more teaching in this area, I recommend that you get that book.

- *Simply Obey God and Practice What His Word Teaches*

You can study and meditate on the Scripture all day long; but, if you do not practice it, it will be useless to you. By practicing it, I mean you simply obey God and do what the Bible teaches, period! For example, the Bible teaches that you should not have sex outside of marriage, so you stop doing that, if you are living in this type of sin. The Bible says you should forgive others who mistreat you; thus you simply forgive, whether or not the transgressor is right or wrong. Additionally, the Bible teaches that we should serve, and emulate Christ; hence, you serve in your local church or in other Christ centered ministries. You would do these things regardless of how you feel, because as Christians, we live by faith and not by how we feel (2 Corinthians 5:7). In addition, you give financially to support God's work; you walk in love and express kindness and compassion towards others; you pray for your enemies; etc. And most importantly, you allow the Holy Spirit to guide your life daily, and you become submissive to His promptings in your heart.

Seeking Godly Counsel

I do realize that a new Christian may have difficulty in approaching the Scripture. Knowing how to decipher the Scriptures correctly is absolutely critical, in order to avoid heresy (i.e., false teaching). This is so because in the Scripture, we have God's prescriptive decrees, which are His direct commandments or specific will for us to practice, such as, but not limited to, witnessing to others; supporting His work on the earth; loving others; etc. Then, there are also descriptive accounts in the Bible, such as, but not limited to, various incidences of murder, jealousy, strife, and a host of evil deeds ignited by Satan himself, which God did not approve of, but these incidences are recorded in the Bible to teach us not to practice them.

Thus, if you are unsure about what certain Scriptures are teaching, do not act on them immediately; instead, seek counsel from a mature Christian who has evidence of "walking" with God in His or her life. As an example, such an individual would know and practice what the Word of God teaches, he or she would be walking in love, peace, joy, and be involved in good service to the Lord, etc. It is important that you are discipled (i.e., taught) how to study and apply the Word of God in your life, so seeking a mature mentor is relevant.

The Christian life is not an event; rather, it is a daily lifestyle. It is impossible to practice true Christianity without the help of the Holy Spirit who indwells each true believer. Thus, as you make Jesus Christ your Lord and submit to all of His teachings in the Bible, while allowing the Holy Spirit to guide you daily, your lifestyle will reflect the presence of God, and God will be glorified. But, to do this, it will be best that you become a living sacrifice; meaning, surrendering your carnal wishes and desires daily, to the Lordship of Christ, and allowing Him preeminence in your life; then you will be able to overcome, and enjoy the blessed life that Jesus died for you to enjoy in this present life (Romans 12:1; John 10:10).

And as you do your best to practice God's Word daily while trusting Him with the results, you will never regret it. This is because God is faithful, and He has told us that we should never give up in practicing godliness, because in due time, we will reap abundantly, if we do not give up (Galatians 6:7-11). Thus, at the right time, the life in the Scriptures (John 6:63), will radiate through you, and you, and others, will take notice. Thus, keep trusting God, and remember, apart from Jesus, you can accomplish nothing! (John 15:5). So, you are safe in the hands of Christ!

Summary Points:

- The initial step in knowing God is to have a sincere desire to want to spend time in His presence, through His Word;
- Taking Scriptures out of context is the primary reason for heresy (false teachings), and the primary reason for the existence of pseudo Christian cults;
- Meditation is essential, in order to obtain revelation from God's Word;
- True Christianity is a lifestyle, requiring a daily submission to the teachings of Christ; allowing the Holy Spirit to guide and direct our lives daily; while obeying God's decrees in the Scriptures.

Points For Consideration:

- What are your thoughts about the biblical Truth that only those who obey God and practice His Word receive His blessings?
- Do you believe God can speak to you directly from His Word? If no, why not?
- What are your thoughts about meditation, for the Christian? Can you see yourself doing it?

Concluding Remarks

The Bible is very clear in teaching that in the beginning, God spoke through the prophets, but today, He has spoken through His Son, Jesus Christ (Hebrews 1:1-2). Additionally, the Bible teaches us that All Scripture is God-breathed, meaning inspired, for purposes of teaching us All Truths pertaining to living godly lifestyles, in order to glorify God in this dark world (2 Timothy 3:16).

It Will Change Your Life

As already explained in this book, there is no human problem, circumstance, condition, etc, that the Bible has not already provided us with the solution. Hence, the Bible has the answers to All of life's issues — no wonder it has remained the number one bestselling book of all time, and it will continue to do so.

Many people criticize the Bible, even though most of them have never taken the time to read through it for themselves. I guarantee you, based on the authority of God's Word, if you were to invest some time in studying the Bible for yourself, you will learn that the critics are wrong, as always; and any so called inconsistencies in the Bible are mostly minor, irrelevant grammatical typos, such as misplaced commas, punctuations, incorrect spellings of words, etc. And these grammatical errors do not affect God's message and/or the key doctrines of true Christianity. Hence, I challenge you, to start studying the Bible today, and you will realize, very quickly, the supernatural unity of God's Word.

In the pages of the Bible, you will find God's perfect will for you, His beloved child. If you agree with Him, and act in accordance with His will for you as outlined in the Scriptures, it will change your life for the better. **God wants the best for you, because He loves you; but, do you want the best for yourself? If yes, the teachings in the Bible offer a step-by-step guide for you to navigate through this dark world. You can trust the Bible.**

If you have never read through the Bible, I hope this book has motivated you enough, so that you can begin studying today. If you want to see godly changes and results in your life, the teachings in the Bible will help you. What do you have to lose? Give God a chance, and it will be the best decision you will ever make! You will not regret it, I guarantee you!

I AM A LIVING TESTIMONY

I am a living testimony that the Word of God works. I have discussed my testimony in another book; but briefly, when I was diagnosed with metastasis colon cancer and given a very dire prognosis, I turned to God 100% as my healer. For a period of about 11- 12 months during the first year of the diagnosis, I spent about 8 to 10 hours a day studying and meditating on God's Word, specifically on the healing Scriptures.

And, without anyone laying hands on me, I received supernatural illumination and/or revelation about God as my healer. That revelation quickened my spirit, strengthened my faith, provided a supernatural peace, hope, and assurance that I was already healed. Today, I am 100% cancer free after almost 9 years. In addition, all of the other diseases I was diagnosed with as a result of the cancer supernaturally disappeared, without any medical intervention — I just focused on the Word of God, which became my medicine. God can do the same for you too! It is up to you, and not God; but remember, He is always willing and available to help!

Besides being healed from cancer, the teachings from the Word of God has transformed my life in every area. Today, as I spend time with God daily, I am walking in His supernatural peace, joy, and strength, and I have been delivered from all sorts of ungodly emotions such as fear, worry, anxiety, which I used to suffer from. I live daily under the Lordship of Jesus Christ, and I depend on the Holy Spirit daily, to guide my life, and He does. I know, beyond a shadow of a doubt, that **God's Word is the Only Absolute Truth,** and I depend and rely on it daily; and I am excelling in Christ —I wish the same for you. But before you can enjoy the best God has for you, you must have a relationship with His only Son, Jesus Christ.

ACCEPT TO FOLLOW JESUS CHRIST NOW

As I have already explained throughout this book, Jesus Christ is God's gift to Mankind. Jesus Christ fulfilled All of the Messianic prophecies 100%. His death, burial and resurrection has paved the way, for us, fallen human beings to have a direct relationship with God, if we so desire. But to have a relationship with God, you must come through the Lord Jesus, because He is The only person in the history of the world, who has met God's perfect standard of holiness 100%. And the Bible teaches us that salvation (i.e., being delivered from our Sinful fallen Natures; from the Kingdom of darkness belonging to Satan; and having a relationship with God through Christ) can only come through one person: Jesus Christ, who died for the sins of the entire world (1 John 2:2; Acts 4:12). Even though Jesus died for the sins of the entire world, each individual, must, by his or her choice, decide to accept His free gift of salvation, in order to enter into a relationship with God the Father.

Having a relationship with God is simple, if you truly believe in your heart that Jesus Christ died for your personal sins, and was raised from the dead on the third day; the Bible teaches that if you believe this, and then confess it with your mouth, you will be saved. Jesus Himself teaches that He is The Only way to God the Father (John 14:6). So, if you are ready to ask Jesus into your life, simply ask Him now, and He will accept (Revelation 3:20). If you need help asking Him, simply say the simple prayer below. Keep in mind the prayer is not what saves you; rather, it is what you believe in your heart, and you are just saying it out of your mouth. Below is the prayer:

Dear God, I acknowledge I am a sinner. I thank you for sending Your Only Son, Jesus Christ to die on the cross for my personal sins. Today, I ask that you forgive me for not acknowledging this before. Today, I ask you Jesus, to come into my life and change me. I have chosen you, as my personal Lord and Savior, and from this day forward, I denounce all other gods in my life. I receive your forgiveness, right now. Also, please fill me with Your Holy Spirit, right now, so that I can learn how to live as Your child. Thank you God for answering this prayer, and by faith, I declare, right now, that I am a Christian, in Jesus name, AMEN!

Friend, if you said that prayer genuinely, based on the authority of God's Word, you are a true Christian, and God's Spirit, the Holy Spirit has instantly sealed you, and you belong to God (Ephesians 1:13). According to Jesus, your personal Lord and Savior, no one will ever snatch you from His hands; your eternity is secured! (John 10:28-29).

Now that you are a Christian, the next thing is for you to start studying God's Word as already discussed in this book. Then, find a Bible believing church in your local area and become a member, and start fellowshipping with other believers and grow in your relationship with God through

Concluding Remarks

Christ. Be certain that you find a church that practices what the Bible teaches, and Jesus is the center of that church, and the power of God, through the Holy Spirit is evident there (I discuss more about the Church in my book: "**Are You Moving Forward with Jesus**...", consider getting this resource, which will help you significantly in your journey with God).

We also ask that you contact us, if you genuinely said that prayer. And remember that we have an audio Podcast series that will help you grow in God's Word, so feel free to subscribe to that, if you so desire. Welcome, into the Kingdom of Light: God's Kingdom, in Jesus name, AMEN.

You can email or contact us:

Dr Ruth Tanyi Ministries, Inc
P O BOX 1806
Loma Linda, CA, 92354, USA
Email: Info@DrRuthtanyi.org

Bibliography

Associated Press article "Wine Jug Bears Herod's Name, " July 9 1996, http://articles.latimes.com/1996-07-09/news/mn-22431_1_wine-jug, accessed February 22, 2015.

Campbell, Charlie L. Archeological Evidence for the Bible. The Always Be Ready Apologetic Ministry, 2012.

Cruse, C. F. Eusebius': Ecclesiastical History. Complete and Unabridged (New Updated Edition). Peabody, MA: Hendrickson Publishers, 1998.

Diego, Mesa. How to Dream When You Are Told You're Going To Die: Cancer Stage 4: It's Just a Number, Dream Releaser Publishing, 2014.

Fox News "2,000-Year-Old Priestly Burial Box Is Real, Archaeologists Say," June 29th 2011, http://www.foxnews.com/scitech/2011/06/29/israeli-scholars-confirm-authenticity-2000-year-old-burial-box-belonging-to/, accessed February 10, 2015.

Fox News "2,000-Year-Old Priestly Burial Box Is Real, Archaeologists Say," June 29th 2011, http://www.foxnews.com/scitech/2011/06/29/israeli-scholars-confirm-authenticity-2000-year-old-burial-box-belonging-to/, accessed February 10, 2015.

F. F. Bruce. The New Testament Documents: Are they Reliable. Grand Rapids : William B. Eerdmans, 1981.

Flavius Josephus, The Antiquities of the Jews, 18:63-64.

Iraq and the Bible. http://www.biblearchaeology.org/post/2005/09/15/Iraq-and-the-Bible.aspx#Article, accessed March 25, 2015.

J. D. Douglas & Merrill C. Tenney (editors). NIV Compact Dictionary of the Bible. Grand Rapids: Zondervan, 1989.

Los Angeles Times " Biblical Pool Uncovered in Jerusalem," August 9, 2005, http://articles.latimes.com/2005/aug/09/science/sci-siloam9, accessed February 5, 2015.

Mauck, J. W. Paul on Trial: The Book of Acts As A Defense of Christianity. Nashville: Nelson, 2001.

Neil R. Lightfoot. How we Got The Bible (3rd edition, Revised and Expanded). Grand Rapids: Baker Books, 2003.

Sproul, R. C. Defending Your Faith: An Introduction to Apologetics. Crossway, 2003.

Tanyi, RA; Berk, LS; Lee JW; Boyd, K., Arechiga, A (2011). The effects of a Psychoneuroimmunology (PNI) based lifestyle intervention in modifying the progression of depression in clinically depressed adults. International Journal of Psychiatry in Medicine, 42(2):151-66.

The Chicago Hittite Dictionary Project. https://oi.uchicago.edu/research/projects/chicago-hittite-dictionary-project, accessed May 10th 2015.

Time magazine "Are the Bible's Stories True? Archaeology's Evidence," December 18, 1995, accessed October 21, 2017.

Soukhanov, et al. The American Heritage Dictionary of the English Language (3rd Edition). Boston: Houghton Mifflin Company, 1996.

Stoner, P.W. & Newman, R. C. Science Speaks. Moody Publishers, 1958.

Walter C. Kaiser Jr. The Old Testament Documents: Are they Reliable and Relevant? Illinois: IVP Academic, 2001.

Walvoord, J. F. Every Prophecy Of the Bible. Colorado Springs, CO: David Cook, 2011.

www.icr.org.

www.jw.org.

www.mormon.org.

www.britannica.com/biography/Saint-Paul-the-Apostle, accessed January 16, 2015.

W. E. Vine, Merrill F. Unger, William White, Jr. Vine's Complete Expository Dictionary of Old and New Testament Words. Nashville: Nelson, 1996.

Whiston W. The Works of Josephus: Complete and Unabridged (New Updated Edition). Peabody, MA: Hendrickson Publishers, 1987.

Yonge, C. D. The Works of Philo. Complete and Unabridged (New Updated Edition). Peabody, MA: Hendrickson Publishers, 1993.

Zacharias, R and Geisler, Norman (General Editors). Who Made God? And Answers to Over 100 Other Tough Questions of Faith. Zondervan, 2003.

OTHER BOOKS BY DR TANYI

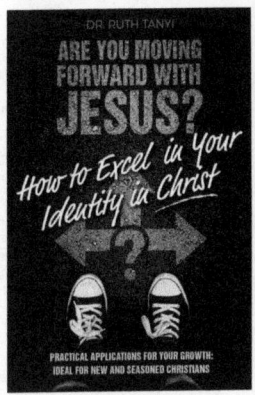
Are You Moving Forward with Jesus? How to Excel In Your Identity in Christ

Answers to the Toughest 25 Questions about the "Real Jesus"

Faith to Receive God's Promises. How to "Walk" in Biblical Faith and Allow the Blessings of God to Chase You

COMING SOON!

13 Reasons why People Get Sick! A Biblical Perspective & Remedies

Did God Really Say that? How to Overcome Doubt and Receive God's Promises: 10 Life-Changing Lessons Learned from Overcoming Metastasis Colon Cancer.

Healed by the Stripes of Jesus: A True Story of God's Unconditional Grace and Love: My Story! My Miracle! How I Overcame Metastasis Colon Cancer: You can Be Healed Too!

AUDIO CD TEACHING LIBRARY

Faith to Receive God's Promises: How to "Walk" in Biblical Faith and Allow the Blessings of God to Chase You

The Heart of True Christianity: The Gospel Message of Jesus Christ: Answers to 10 Major Questions Pertaining to Your Salvation in Christ Jesus

What Are the Gifts of the Spirit?

Holy Spirit-Led Healthy Emotions: The Fruit of the Spirit and Your Health

How to Overcome Doubt and Receive God's Promises

13 Reasons Why People Get Sick: A Biblical Perspective & Remedies

AUDIO CD TEACHING LIBRARY

Unforgiveness and Other Toxic Emotions: How to Walk in Forgiveness

Live Above Your Fears & Overcome Sicknesses and Diseases

Be Anxious No More

Daily Habits For Your Soul

Are You Moving Forward with Jesus? How to Excel In Your Identity in Christ

OTHER TEACHINGS BY DR TANYI

Discipleship Bible Teaching Series

Biblical Preventive Health with Dr Ruth ® Magazine

13 Reasons Why True Christianity is Different: A Wall Mount Poster
A Call to Action Poster

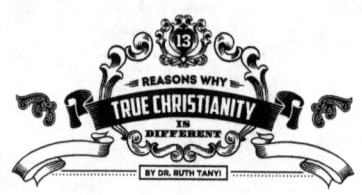

Visit **Dr Ruth Tanyi Ministries YouTube Channel** and watch our FREE Devotional Teachings, Plus Other FREE Teachings at your convenience, 24/7. Subscribe to our YouTube Channel and start enjoying our Free Teachings Today.

Visit www.Drruthtanyi.org/blog and watch our FREE Devotional Teachings.

Obtaining Ministry Resources

To get more information about the above ministry resources, please visit our Website: **www.DrRuthTanyi.org**

Contact Information
You Can also Email or Contact us:

Dr Ruth Tanyi Ministries, Inc
P O BOX 1806
Loma Linda, CA, 92354, USA
Email: Info@DrRuthtanyi.org

ABOUT THE AUTHOR

Dr. Ruth Tanyi, DrPH, NP, ACSM HFS; CNS; MA Ministry

Dr. Ruth Tanyi is a Bible Teacher, Doctor of Preventive Care/Integrative Medicine, Board Certified Nutritionist and Exercise Physiologist. She is the founder /CEO of Dr. Ruth Tanyi Ministries, a non-denominational Christian, non-profit ministry located in San Bernardino, California, with primary focus on spreading the uncompromising Gospel of Jesus Christ; sharing God's unconditional love and grace, while concurrently teaching others how to integrate Bible-based principles with medical lifestyle practices in order to prevent and overcome diseases.

Even before being healed by God from metastasis colon cancer and other diseases in 2009, Dr Ruth felt called by God into ministry. However, since her healing and experiential knowledge and revelation of the love and grace of God, she has become an ardent student and teacher of the Word of God.

Dr Ruth's greatest desire is to tell others about God's unconditional love and grace, which she supernaturally experienced, and to teach individuals the lessons she learnt from God on how she received her healing, thereby helping others to be set free as well. Since God is no respecter of persons, Dr Ruth wants to strengthen others by reminding them that if God can heal her, He (God), can set them free as well regardless of the doctor's diagnosis or prognosis: All things are possible with God.

Dr Ruth is a public speaker and author, and offers a CD and DVD teaching library in addition to books on various topics ranging from the essential doctrines of true Christianity, to teachings on the very essential connection between God's Word and Medicine. Dr Ruth is also actively involved in the Body of Christ via her involvement with other ministries in advancing the Gospel of Jesus Christ, and in espousing the necessity of knowing God's Word. She considers herself to be a non-denominational Bible believing Christian, with a deep desire to fellowship and work with fellow brothers and sisters in Christ, regardless of denominational differences, for the common goal of advancing God's Kingdom and proclaiming the Gospel Message of Jesus Christ in these last days.

Prior to her calling into ministry, she had produced numerous TV series on lifestyle practices and disease prevention which aired throughout Southern California, and are still broadcasting through various media such as True Health Broadcasting Network, and SmartLifestyleTV, a division of LLBN Network worldwide. Her award winning TV series "Bad Sugar"® which focused on Diabetes, in addition to her other TV teachings on lifestyle and disease prevention continues to change thousands of lives.

Dr Tanyi has published numerous academic peer-reviewed journal articles and research papers, and she continues to serve as external reviewer for various International academic peer-reviewed journals. She is still pursuing her academic research in the area of lifestyle practices in preventing and overcoming depression. She has been nominated and selected in WHO IS WHO IN AMERICA and in WHO IS WHO IN Medicine and Healthcare. She is in private practice in San Bernardino California, and lives in Southern California.

For more information visit www.DrRuthTanyi.org, or to contact Dr Tanyi to speak at your event, church or non-Christian event, email her at: DrRuth@DrRuthTanyi.org, or call (909) 383 7978.

www.ingramcontent.com/pod-product-compliance
Lightning Source LLC
LaVergne TN
LVHW041630070426
835507LV00008B/544